State of Transition
Post-Apartheid Educational Reform in South Africa

State of Transition
Post-Apartheid Educational Reform in South Africa

CLIVE HARBER

Monographs in International Education
Series Editors: Colin Brock & Rosarii Griffin

SYMPOSIUM
BOOKS

Symposium Books
PO Box 65 Wallingford, Oxford OX10 0YG, United Kingdom
www.symposium-books.co.uk

Published in the United Kingdom, 2001

ISBN 1 873927 19 3

Typeset in Melior by Symposium Books
Printed and bound in the United Kingdom by Biddles Ltd, *www.biddles.co.uk*

Contents

Preface

All real change involves loss, anxiety and struggle ...
ambivalence will pervade the transition (Fullan, 1991, p. 31)

From 1948 to the early 1990s, South African government was based on an institutionalised system of 'racial' separation and inequality formally known as apartheid. A white minority dominated a black majority in a context of stark social, political and economic differentiation. However, in the late 1980s and early 1990s, the institutions of apartheid began to collapse, leading rapidly to the first South African government based on democratic elections and majority rule in 1994. While the apartheid state used force to maintain this system, formal education was also used to try to make the basic tenets of apartheid 'normal' and 'acceptable' in the minds of South Africans. From the apartheid government's point of view, the role of education was to help to perpetuate and reproduce a racist system and to encourage obedience and conformity to that system. It is not, therefore, surprising that in the 1970s and 1980s education also became a key site in the struggle against apartheid (Kallaway, 1984; Nkomo, 1990; Christie, 1991) or that educational reform was high on the agenda of the first democratically elected government after April 1994.

Indeed, it was clear from the White Paper on *Education and Training* (Department of Education, 1995a) that the new government was aiming at a transformation of education in South Africa. However, this desired transformation will take some time and at the moment it would be more accurate to say that South Africa is in a period of rapid transition. In terms of comparative education, it has been described as a good example of a 'transitology' along with Hungary, Poland, Latvia, the Ukraine, Russia and Iran. This is defined as a situation where over a short time span there occurs the more or less simultaneous collapse and reconstruction of state apparatuses, economic and social stratification systems and the central value system, especially the political value system, to offer a new vision of the future (Cowen, 1999, p. 84). Much of this vision is now relatively clear in South Africa but the processes of implementing the vision remain difficult and problematic.

The main purpose of this book is not to repeat the detailed historical analyses of the development and nature of apartheid education (and the resistance to it) provided in the sources cited earlier, nor to provide a discussion of the political negotiations and processes leading to independence and the first democratic elections, which are best described in Nelson Mandela's own words in *Long Walk To Freedom* (1994). Rather, it is to provide a relatively concise overview of educational transition – to document, discuss and analyse key changes (and continuities) in South African education since the end of apartheid. What makes this period particularly fascinating for educationalists is that the legacy of apartheid and the years of international isolation meant that educational reform had to be fundamental and wide ranging if South Africa was to become a modern, democratic state participating in the global political economy of the twenty-first century. The result was that in the final 5 years of the twentieth century South Africa became something of a laboratory or crucible for educational innovation.

However, while the direction of educational reform has inevitably been strongly influenced by the nature and history of the anti-apartheid struggle inside South Africa, the global political and economic context has also played its part in shaping educational debate and policy and this is reflected in the text. Also, there is a difference between planned reform and the actual nature of educational change on the ground:

> *Transition at the micro-level is much harder to achieve as the*
> *experience of every country engaged in educational transition*
> *as part of a move towards democracy would verify. For, at this*
> *level we are concerned not only with individual schools, but*
> *with individual teachers and pupils within these schools.*
> *(McLeish, 1998, p. 19)*

The book therefore tries where possible to set reform in the contextual realities of South African education as they presently exist in order to understand the difficulties and ambiguities of transition as well as the overt aims and goals as enshrined in policy documents and legislation.

I was in a fortunate position to observe and, in a small way, to participate in the major reforms that were introduced in this period of rapid change. In July 1995 I took a leave of absence from the University of Birmingham to take up a post initially as Head of the Department of Education and then as Head of the School of Education at the University of Natal, Durban. I returned to the UK at the end of March 1999. Since then, I have retained my interest in, and connection with, South Africa through regular visits concerning a research project on schools and violence in Durban.

Given the widespread and multifaceted nature of educational reform in South Africa, the complexity of the South African education system, the length restrictions of the book and my own particular interests and idiosyncrasies, there are inevitably gaps in coverage. I have, for example, largely concentrated on mainstream formal primary and secondary schooling rather than, for example, higher education or on special education. However, I have endeavoured to try to capture the nature of some of the major policy changes and existing realities in relation to economic redress, curriculum and assessment, school and system management, gender and racial equity, teacher education and the conditions of teaching and learning. Finally, it is important to note that use of the terms 'Indian', 'African', 'black', 'coloured' and 'white' do not refer to a fixed or biological concept of 'race' but to the legacy of the social and political system of racial classification of apartheid that still permeates educational debate in South Africa. This being so, I have refrained from using inverted commas in relation to these terms in the text to avoid becoming repetitive.

Clive Harber

Centre for International Education and Research
School of Education, University of Birmingham

CHAPTER 1

Policy, Finance and Governance

Basic Philosophy and Structure

In 1994, the South African people elected a new government, led by the African National Congress (ANC), but consisting of a coalition of other political parties in the interests of national unity. ANC education policy had evolved during the years of struggle against apartheid (Christie, 1991; Harber, 1997a, ch. 10) and had become referred to by the slogan 'People's Education'. Once in government, this very different approach to education had to be clarified and operationalised and the Government of National Unity accordingly produced its first *White Paper on Education and Training* in March 1995. This document marked a radical departure from apartheid education and set out a new philosophy of education for South Africa based on principles of equity and democracy:

> *The realization of democracy, liberty, equality, justice and*
> *peace are necessarily conditions for the full pursuit and*
> *enjoyment of lifelong learning. It should be a goal of education*
> *and training policy to enable a democratic, free, equal, just*
> *and peaceful society to take root and prosper in our land, on*
> *the basis that all South Africans without exception share the*
> *same inalienable rights, equal citizenship and common*
> *destiny, and that all forms of bias (especially racial, ethnic*
> *and gender) are dehumanizing. (Department of Education,*
> *1995a, p. 22)*

That this new philosophy based on democracy and human rights would mean changing all aspects of the education system was also recognised:

> *The letter and spirit of these rights and freedoms should*
> *inform the intellectual culture in all schools and educational*
> *institutions, and professional services in departments of*
> *education. This has unavoidable implications for curricula,*
> *textbooks, other educational materials and media*

> *programmes, teaching methods, teacher education,*
> *professional supervision and management culture.*
> *(Department of Education, 1995a, p. 43)*

The attempt to implement this philosophy and the obstacles and issues that have arisen are the main concerns of this book.

In line with the change of philosophy, the national state structures of apartheid education also had to be dismantled immediately. Under apartheid there were 19 education departments catering for the different racial and ethnic groups. White education was controlled by the white House of Assembly, Indian education by the Indian House of Delegates, coloured education by the coloured House of Representatives and African education in urban areas by the Department of Education and Training. Each African ethnic 'homeland' also had its own education system. After 1994 responsibility for education was divided between the national Ministry of Education and the nine new provinces – Eastern Cape, Free State, Gauteng, KwaZulu Natal, Mpumalanga, Northern Cape, Northern Province, North West and Western Cape. While the South African Constitution and the 1996 Education Act specify the powers and responsibilities of both the national ministry and the provinces in regard to education, it became clear during the first parliament (1994–99) that in practice there is considerable ambiguity and lack of clarity about the roles of the two levels of government. There are therefore regular disagreements and also regular criticisms of some provinces' inability to deliver national education policy. The issue of 'right-sizing' and the redeployment of teachers, which is discussed later, is a case in point. The Minister of Education's quarterly report to parliament at the end of 1999, for example, focused strongly on the provinces and signalled a new intention to intervene more strongly in the future in order to make the provinces function more effectively (Gardiner, 1999).

The Context of Economic Ideology

Education policy does not exist in an economic vacuum. The economic context of educational reform has an important bearing on the nature of policy that has emerged and the way it has been implemented. As in a number of other neighbouring African countries such as Zimbabwe, Namibia and Mozambique, colonialism was associated with capitalism and the respective national independence movements adopted a socialist discourse. Through the years of struggle in the 1970s and 1980s, the ANC espoused socialist policies involving nationalisation of industries and a major role for state intervention in the economy. However, by the late 1980s and early 1990s, the collapse of the Soviet Union and the Communist systems of eastern Europe had begun to change thinking in those African nationalist movements, such as Swapo (the South West Africa People's Organisation) in Namibia and the Eritrean People's

Liberation Front (EPLF) in Eritrea, that were on the verge of taking power. These developments, plus the experience of exile in state-controlled African economies such as those in Zambia and Tanzania, had also begun to force the ANC to rethink its economic policies. The 1994 election campaign was fought on the policy of the Reconstruction and Development Plan (RDP), a basically Keynesian set of policies that would use redistributive taxation to publicly finance an improvement of the basic needs of people – jobs, land, housing, water, electricity, transport, health care and social provision.

However, in June 1996, the Government announced its new macro-economic strategy document called 'Growth, Employment and Redistribution' (GEAR). This was widely seen as a shift away from the Keynesian/welfarist emphasis of the RDP to a neo-liberal strategy of privatisation, ending government subsidies and a reduction in the fiscal deficit through cuts in public spending, including increased introduction of user fees to subsidise public provision. It signalled a reduced role for the state and a greater role for markets and private provision.

There were a number of reasons for this change in economic policy. One is the global dominance of free market ideas and international trends towards privatisation reinforced by the influential advisory role of the World Bank and the International Monetary Fund in South Africa, the major global harbingers of neo-liberal economic policies through their structural adjustment policies. Another reason has been the need for the Government to be seen as 'respectable' and 'responsible' in the eyes of world currency markets, especially in a situation where there has been a 50% devaluation of the rand since 1995.

Nevertheless, whilst the shift to the political right in economic thinking took place relatively rapidly, the ideological traditions of the ANC and its traditional constituencies, plus the glaring levels of inequality and social need, have not meant the adoption of neo-liberal economic ideology in any simple or direct manner. Rather, there is a tension at the heart of government policy between a social democratic and egalitarian philosophy and a competitive, market-driven philosophy. This tension is reflected in debates surrounding educational reform. On the one hand, a financial magazine commenting on South Africa's move to 'cautious Thatcherism' nevertheless noted that 'It is significant, too, that monetary and fiscal disciplines are to be tightened gradually and there still seems to be a radical policy towards the implementation of welfare schemes, especially in education and health' (*Financial Mail*, 21 June 1996). On the other hand, a book on education after apartheid claimed that 'the master narrative of educational reform has, to a large extent, been framed by the international neo-liberal guidelines of the World Bank and the International Monetary Fund' (Kallaway et al, 1997, p. 1).

Finance and Redistribution

However, if education had been entirely framed by World Bank priorities since 1994, the evidence from other countries suggests that education spending would have fallen (Graham-Brown, 1991; Samoff, 1994). In fact, in contrast to World Bank priorities, spending on education has increased strongly since 1995 – growing by 35% up to 1998 (Chisholm & Petersen, 1999), with education's share of the budget growing from 21.9% in 1988/89 to about 28% in both 1998 and 1999, also a relatively high proportion internationally (*Reconstruct*, 14 February 1999; *The Mercury*, 12 March 1998). More is spent on education than any other budgetary item. Even this, however, has not kept up with the needs of an expanding system and the need to achieve greater equity. The historical legacy of apartheid has left a situation of major educational inequalities between different racial groups. In 1988/89, for example, while 656 rand per capita were spent on African children, 1221 rand were spent on coloured children, 2077 rand were spent on Indian children and 2882 rand were spent on white children (Christie, 1991, p. 108). It has been calculated that it would require an increase in the education budget of 144% to raise the level of spending on all schools to that of the previously white schools (Greenstein, 1995, pp. 4–5). The net result is enormous disparities between schools in terms of access to resources, with many schools having, for example, no electricity, clean water or inside toilets while others have audio-visual centres and state-of-the-art computers.

Policy has therefore reflected the ideological tensions described in the preceding section – how to spread existing resources more equitably while looking to alternative private resources for schools. In terms of redistribution, a governmental decision was made to end unequal spending on education by the year 2000. To this end, in 1996 it was agreed between the Government and the teaching unions that class sizes would be set nationally at 1:35 for all secondary schools and 1:40 for all primary schools. In order to achieve this, a major shift in funding and a major redeployment of teachers from richer to poorer provinces would take place. This important experiment in 'right-sizing', as it became known, had two prongs – redeployment of teachers from overstaffed, wealthy schools to poorer rural and township schools, and voluntary severance packages (VSPs) to release from the system teachers who were not willing to be redeployed. The VSPs would be linked to staffing cuts in those provinces deemed to have an oversupply of teachers (Gauteng, Western Cape, Free State and Northern Cape). Limits to geographical mobility caused by family and other circumstances would inevitably mean some teachers taking early retirement and others leaving the profession, but overall the number of teachers was to remain the same. In practice, this policy proved very difficult and controversial to implement.

Predictably, there were protests by parents and teachers in those provinces that would lose staff. However, Garson (1998a) describes the execution of the rationalisation and redeployment process itself as 'nothing less than disastrous'. The lack of capacity and administrative experience in the provinces meant that instead of VSPs being used selectively, some 16,000 teachers were granted them, even in provinces where there was a shortage of teachers and in curriculum areas such as mathematics and science where there are teacher shortages. The net cost ran into millions of rands. Teachers placed on redeployment lists waiting for new posts continued to draw salaries. Meanwhile, schools lacking key personnel, due partly to the numbers taking VSPs, began to employ temporary teachers. Thus, a 'double parking' situation arose and provinces found themselves paying two teachers for the same post. The number of teachers nationally therefore rose from 360,000 to 400,000 and the salary bill continued to rise. At the same time, little real redeployment was taking place as teachers resisted being moved around 'like pawns on a chess table'.

Another blow to the policy was added by Grove Primary School in Cape Town, which took the state to court on the basis that the redeployment policy contravened the 1996 South African Schools Act, which legislated on the organisation, governance and funding of schools. This important Act involved a significant move towards decentralisation in South African education and gave school governing bodies considerable power over the running of schools. The school argued that the redeployment policy undermined the power of governing bodies to appoint their own teachers, forcing them instead to hire teachers on redeployment lists whether or not they were suitable for the job. The court ruled in favour of Grove School and by late 1997 this attempt at redress of past inequalities was at an end. The case clearly highlighted the tension in government policy between decentralisation (a policy consistently favoured by the World Bank and further discussed later) and the need for a more equitable distribution of resources nationally which could only be achieved by centralised directive from the Department of Education.

From January 2000, a new school funding policy (the Norms and Standards Funding Policy) was implemented but applies to non-personnel expenditure only. The policy is to create a uniform funding policy for all provinces and to remove inequities in the distribution of public resources to education. It is also intended to effect redress by introducing poverty-related criteria for the allocation of funds to schools. However, while this policy is an attempt at redistribution, Gardiner (1999) has criticised the policy in terms of its limited impact of the actual funds available for redistribution and the capacity of provincial education departments to implement the policy. In the Western Cape, for example, the worst off schools will receive R196 per pupil per annum and the most affluent will get R28. These funds can only be used for non-personnel purposes and, as Gardiner says, 'It seems clear that with these amounts, the balance will not be swung decisively in favour of those who, historically, have had least'. In the Western Cape, officials developed a formula based on socio-economic and physical variables to distribute funding and came up with 11 categories of school, each containing 9% of the province's learners. A senior education official was asked how it was possible for a primary school in a particular area to be classified as B (acute socio-economic need and inadequate physical facilities) whereas the high school in the same area was classified as F (the norm or centre of the range). It appears that there were insufficient formerly 'white' schools to fill the three most affluent categories, so disadvantaged schools were used at random to top those categories up.

However, at the same time that efforts have been made to redistribute resources from the rich to the poor, there has also been an acceptance that some of the funding burden will have to be borne by users of education in the form of fees. The South African Schools Act permitted the governing bodies of all state schools to levy fees after a majority vote at a meeting of parents, and most now do so. This can be interpreted either as a pragmatic recognition that the state did not have sufficient resources to provide a sufficiently good quality education for all or as further evidence of acceptance of the global influence of the World Bank's agenda of shifting the balance of funding for education from the public to the private sphere. It was certainly the case that in a situation where resources were to be redistributed, the Government accepted the advice of two international consultants that there was a danger of a flight of middle-class parents from the state to the private sector if traditionally advantaged schools were not allowed to raise further resources. This would result in the state sector losing the financial, managerial and persuasive capacities of the better educated and financially advantaged segment of the population (Department of Education, 1996, p. 34). Whatever the explanation, the result will be to exacerbate inequality rather than to reduce it. Schools serving well-off communities can charge high fees to maintain excellent facilities and employ more teachers while schools in poorer communities will not be able to do so. Admission on the grounds of race may now be illegal but high fees may well have the same net effect. It seems very likely that public schools will be increasingly divided between a minority of relatively affluent and well-resourced schools and a majority of poorer schools much more dependent on state funding.

One study of the introduction of school fees in a sample of 26 primary schools and three secondary schools in the Durban area (Azuma, 1999) highlights continuing inequality. Azuma found that in 1998 the average annual fees in ex-KwaZulu Department and Culture (KDEC African) schools was R86, in ex-Department of Education and Training

(DET African) schools it was R90, in ex-House of Delegates (HOD Indian) it was R208, in ex-House of Representatives (HOR coloured) it was R225 and in ex-House of Assembly (HOA white) it was R2791. In the three secondary schools studied the fees at the ex-KDEC were R100, at the ex-HOD school they were R220 and at the ex-HOA school they were R4500. While expenditure at non-ex-HOA primary schools varied between R15,400 and R191,434, expenditure at the three ex-HOA schools was R513,250, R585,000 and R1,356,250. Taking all the primary and secondary schools together, the four ex-HOA schools could afford to hire an extra 50 teachers whereas the other 22 schools could only hire an extra 13 between them. The pupil/teacher ratios in the primary schools varied between 65:1 in the ex-KDEC schools and 27.8:1 in the ex-HOA schools.

Azuma refers to this situation as the 'semi-privatisation' of the public school sector as the price of commodities (in this case education) is increasingly determined by supply and demand in the market. The level of fees is now specified by individual schools and schools compete against each other to attract students on the basis of fees and the perceived standard of education being offered. However, the historical legacy is such that this 'competition' or consumer 'choice' does not take place on an equal basis and Azuma provides evidence that ex-HOA schools are increasingly similar to independent schools in their ability and willingness to attract pupils who live at a considerable distance from the school.

Decentralisation

Decentralisation of power and control has become something of a mantra in international debates on development. Indeed, as USAID notes, it is often treated as a panacea in Africa to solve broader social, political and economic problems as well as educational ones (USAID, 1997, p. vii). Perhaps it is no coincidence that it is also a favoured policy of the World Bank and most countries in sub-Saharan Africa have a structural adjustment programme. However, while decentralisation may be a more efficient way of managing schools, in itself it is in the end merely a mechanism. The question is, efficient at what? Which educational goals is it helping to achieve? In 1991, with the approach of the first democratically elected government, the National Party Government in the all-white House of Assembly significantly decentralised power by creating what it termed 'model c' schools in which white staff and parents would have more control over the running of the school. It was widely felt that this decentralisation of power was negative in intention and was aimed at giving all-white schools some measure of independence to protect their resources and admissions policies from future majority government control.

The South African Schools Act of 1996 also represents a significant move towards decentralisation, although the purpose is very different from that of the previous National Party Government, i.e. to develop an accountable and democratically governed school system based on partnership between government, schools and local communities (Department of Education, 1997a). All public (state) schools must now have a school governing body composed of parents, teachers, learners and non-teaching staff, though the Act stipulates that there must be one more parent on the governing body than the combined total of the other members – parents must be in the majority. Among the powers of the school governing bodies are:

- the adoption of a code of conduct;
- deciding on school times;
- control and maintenance of school property, buildings and grounds;
- recommending and offering advice on the employment of educators and non-educator staff paid for by the state;
- administration of the school fund into which all school fees and donations are made and the preparation of a school budget (including the employment of extra staff); and
- admissions and language policy within the terms of the Act and the constitution.

Sayed (1999) has traced this commitment to decentralisation to grass-roots mobilisation in the struggle against apartheid when the state was the primary apparatus of oppression. Decentralisation and grass-roots community control was therefore the antithesis of state control. However, in line with the privatisation or marketisation of schooling mentioned earlier, he also argues that the South African Schools Act abandons the model of citizenship on which this tradition of parent as citizen is based. This 'left' form of citizenship is where the individual is viewed as self-reliant and not hostage to the state and where the emphasis is on the citizen who works in civil society for the public good and the assertion of civic virtue. Sayed argues that instead, the Act makes parents the primary clients because of their responsibility to pay fees and their majority position on the school governing body. The operation of the market in education creates a conception of the consumer citizen who is a self-interested, utility-maximising, rational individual. The school community becomes the locus for the 'self-interested behaviour of the individual driven toward competition and the acquisition of marketable credentials' (p. 147). Others have cast doubts about whether many working-class and rural black parents will be in a position to participate given that many parents live far from the schools their children attend and therefore face significant transport and time constraints. Also, without appropriate capacity building (promised by the Act), parents from poorer areas may not be able to contribute to effective school management.

Democratisation

In line with the philosophy of education set out in the 1995 White Paper on *Education and Training*, an important further aim of the decentralisation of the Schools Act was the democratisation of schooling:

> *A school governance structure should involve all stake holder*
> *groups in active and responsible roles, encourage tolerance,*
> *rational discussion and collective decision-making.*
> *(Department of Education, 1996, p. 16)*

The policy of school democratisation emerged only gradually from the struggle against apartheid. During and after the Soweto uprising of 1976, the slogan that described opposition education policy was 'liberation first, education later'. While there were demands for greater equality in terms of the distribution of educational resources:

> *White education was not itself subjected to a critique.*
> *Thus, for example, its undemocratic organisation, its*
> *individualistic orientation, its internal inequalities, its elitism*
> *and its methods of teaching were never questioned ... the*
> *major thrust was a rejection of Bantu education with little or*
> *nothing being said about an alternative education system.*
> *(Wolpe, 1995, p. 23)*

It was an authoritarian and rigidly hierarchical educational system as well as a racist one. As Christie put it:

> *If you go into any school – white or black – you'll soon know*
> *who is in charge. There is a ladder of seniority, with the*
> *principal at the top, then deputy principals and vice*
> *principals, then senior teachers, then ordinary staff. You can*
> *even tell this hierarchy from the position and size of their*
> *offices and where they sit in the staff room. Somewhere at the*
> *bottom of the hierarchy are the students. But even amongst the*
> *students there is hierarchy as well – prefects, senior students*
> *etc. (1991, p. 46)*

I asked postgraduate initial teacher education students at the University of Natal who attended school during the apartheid years to write about their own experience of schooling in relation to democracy and authoritarianism. The following two quotations are examples of the general trend:

> *My personal experience of school education was authoritarian*
> *to say the least. As is the case with most authoritarian*

> *institutions, there was a hierarchical leadership, beginning with the principal at the top and the students at the bottom. Somewhere in between were the teachers and parents. As for student representatives, there were none. The only student leadership roles were for prefects and even then they were there to enforce the rules made by the principal and staff ... The students were merely objects and education, sadly, was aimed at simply replacing the previous generation with a mirror image of itself.*

> *I remember my school experience at a secondary school in KwaZulu Natal. The headteacher of that school could scold at his assistant teachers in front of the students. And if a student committed a minor offence, like arriving late at school, could get up to ten strokes on the back without bothering to find out why she or he was late. She or he would then be ordered to crawl on knees up the classroom ... These practices were not exceptional in my school. I remember that whenever students from different schools met the issue of students' beating was discussed.*

More democratic and participatory notions of education began to emerge within the democratic movement in South Africa through discussions surrounding the nature of 'People's Education' as an alternative to apartheid education (Christie, 1991; Chisholm & Fuller, 1996; Soobrayan, 1998) and outside South Africa through practice at the ANC school for political exiles near Morogoro in Tanzania (Serote, 1992; Harber, 1997a, ch. 10).

By the time the ANC-led government came to power in 1994, such discussions and experience were influential not only in shaping policy within the ANC but were also part of a wider international agenda and discourse on education, democracy and human rights that had strengthened and grown since the end of the cold war in the late 1980s (Harber, 1997b). Consequently, in 1995, when the Minister of Education established a Committee to Review the Organisation, Governance and Funding of Schools, the committee commissioned Sibusiso Sithole of the Durban Education Policy Unit to write a discussion paper on the participation of students in democratic school governance, in which he traced experience of student participation both nationally and internationally (Canada, United Kingdom, New Zealand, Australia, Mozambique and Namibia) and argued that power and decision-making inside secondary schools should be shared with learners and that learners should be represented on school governing bodies. It has been argued that this was influential in the drafting of the South African Schools Act in relation to the participation of students in school management (Sithole, 1998).

The South African Schools Act subsequently legislated that all secondary schools must have an elected representative council of learners, which must itself elect students onto the school governing body, where they participate in decisions as full members. Such councils and school governing bodies have now been established in most secondary schools but unfortunately, as yet, there is little data on how they are actually functioning. Certainly, those researching the establishment of democratic structures have expressed concern at signs of a lack of knowledge of legislated functions and an incapacity to perform functions without more capacity building and training (Karlsson et al, 1999) and there are signs of some confusion and tension between the responsibilities of parents and educators in the running of the schools. Nevertheless, the introduction of such democratic structures can, as the legislation intends, provide a framework for the development of more democratic values and behaviours within the school and the wider society, including those associated with anti-racism. A case study of ways in which this might be achieved will be discussed in the next chapter. However, as the case study makes clear, the structures must be effectively established and go hand in hand with an energetic attempt to change the behavioural culture of the school in a democratic direction – the rules, daily practices and interpersonal relations that constitute the lived reality of the school, i.e. how people actually treat one another.

One obstacle to the creation of a more democratic environment in schools is the use of corporal punishment. Authority based on fear and violence is hardly compatible with a democratic school ethos of open dialogue and mutual respect. Section 12 of the South African Constitution states that everyone has the right not to be treated or punished in a cruel, inhuman or degrading way and the South African Schools Act has also therefore made corporal punishment in schools illegal. However, it is a practice deeply and widely supported amongst parents, teachers and even learners and is still embedded in many South African schools, as chapter 4 of this book will show.

AIDS and Education

Sadly, any discussion of the policy context of education in South Africa must also recognise the potential impact of the AIDS epidemic facing the country. Among girls between 15 and 19 years of age, the rate of HIV infection rose from 12.7% in 1997 to 21% in 1998, while the rate for women of 20 attending antenatal clinics rose from 17 to 22% in the same period (Badcock-Walters, 2000). In KwaZulu Natal, a province particularly affected by the epidemic, a health department survey in 1998, for example, found that 35.2% of the population was infected, with the bulk of cases involving people between 15 and 25 (Pillay, 2000a). As one commentary on the new Minister of Education's priorities put it:

> *Many of Minister Asmal's visions for education simply cannot happen within the context of a major HIV/AIDS epidemic. Likewise, many of the gains he envisages for society through improvement in the education system will achieve very little if the HIV infection rate remains high. An uncontrolled and misunderstood epidemic, as we have now, has the potential to undermine completely all the developmental gains that South Africa is hoping to make through improved education [yet] ...To date there is very little to indicate that any planning is being done that seriously considers the possible demographic and financial effects of AIDS on the education sector. (Motala et al, 1999, p. 29)*

There are a number of potentially important ramifications of the AIDS epidemic for education. Teachers will face increasing infection and death, with pupil–teacher ratios worsening as teachers fall ill and die. In Zambia, for example, deaths of teachers in-service are already the equivalent to the loss of about two-thirds of the total output of the country's teacher training colleges (Pillay, 2000b). Moreover, other categories of educational staff are also likely to be affected – ground staff, cleaning staff and educational administrators. The limited resources available to education will be affected by the health benefits available to infected staff, the cost of replacement staff to cover sick leave absences and the cost of teacher training to replace those who die. On the other hand, pupil attendance could be affected by the need for long periods of home nursing, agricultural labour or because there is no money for education. This will have a problematic effect on educational planning in terms of how many classrooms, textbooks and teachers will be needed. Finally, there will be the problem of attitudes and behaviour towards those ill with AIDS and still within the education system.

One writer on the relationship between AIDS and education has commented that:

> *While no simple solution offers itself, it is clear that the problem is as much a state of official and public mindset as it is a level of physical infection. Given the unique opportunity presented by the education system to play a central role in reduction and prevention, it is extraordinary that it has not only been ignored but that the sector has been allowed to become a major part of the problem. (Badcock-Walters, 2000)*

Yet, one indicator of the obstacles to be overcome occurred when half of a group of 200 teachers walked out of an HIV awareness lecture because they were offended and embarrassed by the graphic nature of the material. The lecture was part of a Gauteng Department of Education project to educate educators about HIV/AIDS as part of the Government's Curriculum 2005 reform, discussed in more detail in chapter 3. Lecturers on the project said that on some occasions there had been 100% walkouts. As one of the remaining teachers put it, 'How can we expect to teach our children about the realities of a national crisis when we want to ignore those realities ourselves?' (Dyanti, 1999). This is a pertinent reminder of the role of contextual realities in the difficult process of moving from policy to practice, a key and recurring theme of this book.

Conclusion

The policy context for South African educational reform reflects the different and contradictory influences on the ANC-led Government. On the one hand, the history of the ANC within South Africa has been one of struggle for equity, social justice and democracy. These strands are clearly represented in educational policy via attempts at redistribution from the richer to the poorer sections of the community and through the introduction of democratic structures into all secondary schools. However, the sanctioning of user fees in combination with decentralisation will almost certainly preserve and even exacerbate inequalities and some inevitably see the global hegemony of neo-liberal economics and the behind the scenes influence of the World Bank as the main cause. It is likely that this tension in educational policy will persist for the foreseeable future as the Government tries to balance demands for redistribution and greater justice on the one hand with the need to maintain existing and traditional levels of perceived quality on the other. Darkly overshadowing all efforts at reform, however, is the potential impact of the growing AIDS epidemic in South Africa. This is something that educationalists can ill afford to ignore for very much longer.

CHAPTER 2

Over the Rainbow?
Race, Language and Gender

Introduction

It is impossible and even dangerous to separate education from values. Highly 'educated', or at least qualified, people have been responsible for major atrocities in recent human history, often associated with forms of racism. The Truth and Reconciliation Commission in South Africa, for example, noted that medical doctors were implicated in cases of torture under the apartheid regime. Learning and qualifications can be put to good or evil ends and schools should therefore pay serious attention to the social and political values that accompany the acquisition of knowledge and skills.

The 1995 *White Paper on Education and Training* therefore cites the preamble to the 1993 South African Constitution on the:

> *need to create a new order in which all South Africans shall be entitled to a common South African citizenship in a sovereign and democratic constitutional state in which there is equality between men and women and people of all races so that all citizens shall be able to exercise their fundamental rights and freedoms. (Department of Education, 1995a, p. 39)*

The Bill of Rights of the South African Constitution explicitly forbids either the state or individuals to discriminate against anyone on the grounds of race, gender, pregnancy, marital status, ethnic or social origin, colour, sexual orientation, age, disability, religion, conscience, belief, culture, language or birth. Under the Prevention and Prohibition of Unfair Discrimination Bill introduced in 2000, racist and sexist remarks and behaviour would be punishable by fines as part of a legal framework for dealing with discriminatory behaviour (Randall, 1999).

The philosophical, constitutional and legislative position is therefore clear – racism, sexism and other contraventions of human rights should have no part to play in the new South Africa. As government publications on education have also made clear, schooling should be at the forefront in the elimination of such prejudice and discrimination. This chapter examines progress in education in relation to racism and sexism.

Racism

One cannot expect distrust, suspicion and hatred to
be replaced instantly by trust and warm embraces.
(Naidoo, 1996, p. 84)

The progress of desegregation has certainly begun but it is a one-way process, with African students going to formerly all-white or Indian schools. African schools remain 'as mono-racial as ever' (Wedekind et al, 1996, p. 424). By mid-1995, for example, it was estimated that the number of African students at formerly white schools did not exceed 12–15% (Chisholm, 1995, p. 7). However, desegregation has not been welcomed everywhere. The South African Rights Commission in KwaZulu Natal has argued that high school fees are being used as a mechanism to exclude certain communities that cannot afford to pay and that this is a form of 'mutant racism' (Broughton, 2000). Less subtle has been the active resistance to desegregation in some Afrikaans medium schools. One case which caused much media attention was that of the Potgietersrus Primary School where the Education Department of the Northern Province took the school's governing body to court because of its refusal to admit black pupils. Another was Vryburg High School in the North West Province where black students were put into the school hall and left there for 3 weeks without receiving any teaching. Many left the school during the course of the year.

However, while there have been a number of other such schools, some leading to violent conflict between black and white pupils, and there is evidence that a significant minority of white teachers were opposed to integration (Skuy & Vice, 1996), the key problem in the majority of schools is not overt resistance to desegregation but a failure to address change and promote integration. Simply putting students from different racial backgrounds into the same school is not the same as then trying to alter the nature of the relationships between students and between staff and students. This requires positive attempts to foster a school climate and individual behaviour based on trust, mutual acceptance and respect, and equality with diversity. In a society marked by racism, a failure to actively intervene has the net effect of reproducing racism (or sexism) by default or omission.

However, in Naidoo's (1996) study of 26 desegregated schools in KwaZulu Natal he found that the dominant attitude was 'business as usual' and little thought had been given to changing the structures, policies and practices of schools so that they could handle and build on the new diversity. Many teachers and principals felt ill equipped to deal with racism because it is a difficult and sensitive issue for which they had had no training or under apartheid had actually been trained in racism. The tendency was, therefore, to ignore racial incidents or see them as other forms of conflict or anti-social behaviour. As a result, many African students perceived their schools to be ignoring racism, and lacked confidence and trust in them. One learner, for example, said that:

> When we complain about not being treated right, they feel we
> are demanding. They say we must change and not the school.
> If there are any fights and so on we just have to listen to the
> principal and forget about what has happened. They don't try
> to find the real cause of the problem. Like sometimes the other
> pupils and some teachers are racist. (Naidoo, 1996, p. 76)

South African writing on race and education has been very influenced by United Kingdom writing on the same topic and three approaches to race relations in the school stemming from this literature are regularly used to analyse the situation in South Africa. A common approach is assimilation, where the burden is placed on those coming into the school to adopt the values and lifestyle of the existing or dominant group. Race and diversity is ignored on the assumption that all will conform to a given and established pattern of traditions, rules and structures. A multicultural approach, on the other hand, recognises and even celebrates cultural difference and includes examples of diversity in the curriculum, such as a comparison between Hindu, Christian and Zulu festivals. This approach is perhaps best captured in the phrase 'the rainbow nation', widely used at the time of the 1994 election to promote a sense of belonging and inclusion for all racial and ethnic groups at a time when there were serious worries about inter-group violence and conflict. However, the problem with a multicultural approach is that it also gives the impression that cultures are static and homogeneous and fails to address the issue of racism or the use of power by one racial group to maintain their socio-economic and political advantage over others by forms of direct and indirect discrimination. A third approach, anti-racism, builds on multiculturalism by acknowledging and analysing the existence of racism and actively challenging it through school rules and the curriculum.

Carrim (1998) uses these categories to trace patterns of desegregation in South African schools during the period 1990–96, particularly in relation to the Gauteng region. In 1990–94, the approach was essentially assimilationist, with students coming into the white, Indian or coloured schools expected to adapt to the existing cultural ethos. The teachers made consistent reference to an 'us' and 'them' language and the more 'they' become like 'us' the more acceptable 'they' become. Nevertheless, while the dominant approach remained one of assimilation, the daily contact with multilingual, multiethnic and multiracial classrooms began to push teachers to a more multicultural approach as they were at least forced to recognise the different backgrounds and experiences of the 'others'. However, this tentative multiculturalism tended to be negative and based on narrow, fixed and homogeneous cultural stereotypes and even caricatures of lifestyles. Carrim argues that such approaches by teachers fail to recognise the power and material dimensions of racism and fail to reduce racist practices or instances of racial abuse. Yet, as he points out:

> There is no nationally instituted anti-racist programme or package which has been put into place. There are no structured, co-ordinated programmes to help teachers cope with multiracial/cultural/lingual/ability classrooms. There are no nationally or provincially co-ordinated programmes for students to develop anti-racist, anti-sexist, anti-discrimination awareness or consciousness in the formal workings of the school. It is almost as if these are expected to occur almost entirely of their own accord. (1998, p. 318)

In June 1998, the Education Policy Unit of the University of Natal conducted a snap telephone survey of almost one hundred schools across five provinces. The data collected confirmed that about 80% of desegregated public schools in South Africa were pursuing an ad hoc and reactive approach with no significant support from provincial departments of education. Research by Zafar (1998) in KwaZulu Natal that set out to identify case studies of good practice in using proactive anti-racist strategies in schools also found very little evidence of such an approach. The evidence therefore overwhelmingly points to assimilation being the dominant response to desegregation in South African schools.

What is the effect on the attitudes of young people? Incidents of racial conflict and violence at a number of Afrikaans medium schools have indicated persistent levels of racism amongst white students. At Schweizer-Reneke Highschool, for example, a group of 35 white students assaulted a group of 20 black students with cricket bats, sticks and wooden planks. Four black students were hospitalised. Interviews with black and white students revealed considerable racial tension. Interviews with white students produced the following comments:

> Black students must just leave us alone and not mix with us. I would be happy if they [the black students] were taken to another school. My parents say the same thing. They know what they are talking about and I listen to them.

I have a problem with black students. I don't want them to
speak to me because I hate them.

Another student said he would leave if black teachers were employed at the school (Ratshitanga, 1998).

However, even more worrying was the result of a recent and very important South African Human Rights Commission Report of an audit of 90 desegregated schools across all nine provinces (Vally & Dalamba, 1999). The report showed that racism in schools was pervasive. They summarised the situation as follows:

In fact little progress has been made to ensure an end to racial
discrimination and prejudice in schools. Our Commission has
had to deal with a large number of complaints: discrimination
in disciplinary measures, racial violence and cultural
prejudice. Schools continue to be characterised by racial
separation and discrimination. Efforts at racial integration
have not achieved the desired results because learners
approach school with the prejudices imbued in their home
environments and the schools have no mechanisms to
challenge and stimulate the unlearning of ingrained
prejudices, as well as transform the minds of learners.
Educators exhibit little or no commitment to constructing a
learning environment free from discrimination and prejudice.
Too many prefer to deny the existence of racism or presume a
superficial tolerance. Some prefer to have their schools as
laboratories for cultural assimilation where black learners
are by and large tolerated rather than affirmed as of right.
Four years after the miracle of 1994, school playgrounds
are battlegrounds between black and white schoolgoers.
(1999, Preface)

Data obtained from questionnaires directed at senior students and school management were supplemented by interviews with teachers, principals and senior learners. When asked, 'Have there been racial incidents or examples of racism in your school', 62% answered yes. Almost 60% of learners felt that their schools did not have a policy/programme to eliminate racism or that it is unsuccessful. Teachers in the schools remain overwhelmingly white: 78% were white, 13% Indian, 7% coloured and 2% African. Examples of racist comments and negative stereotyping from students (Indian and coloured as well as white) are provided in detail in the report. Racism is so common in these schools that it takes on a sort of 'normality':

Hundreds of respondents regard racism as part of their
everyday experience. It is manifested in rhetoric, name-calling,
stereotyping, labels and anxieties in the classroom, corridors,

29

*playgrounds and extracurricular events. Often racialisation is
expressed when displays of masculinity become associated
with the ability to use racially abusive language and where the
exclusion of some learners from (for example) certain sports
serves to signify masculine and racialised dominance. (p. 59)*

While most teachers were generally supportive of black learners, they
did feel frustrated by the lack of systemic intervention in the form of
anti-racist training in the schools. (The schools were again
overwhelmingly assimilationist in their approach and not one example
of an anti-racist approach was discovered.) Nevertheless:

*Learners report some instances where teachers are insulting
and abusive, using unacceptable and highly demotivating and
derogatory language. Learners talk of enduring this abuse for
fear of victimisation by teachers and the complicity of some
principals. (p. 56)*

Even school buildings and decor can play a part:

*Many of the traditionally white Afrikaans schools promote
symbols which thoroughly alienate black learners. Instances
include the display of the old South African flag in the
principal's office, dominant sports codes such as rugby in
areas where black people do not play this sport, bas-reliefs of
the Great Trek and intimidating portraits of earnest white men
adorning school halls. (pp. 27–28)*

One of the authors of the report stated that he was 'appalled by the
intensity and prevalence of racist and violent thinking' and noted that
the Department of Education has:

*paid very little attention to the human side, to the social
relations at school level. The particular atmosphere at school
lends itself to these violent outpourings of racism, sexual
harassment, suicide and shootings. There is just not enough
counselling and care in a hostile world. (Garson, 1999)*

The report makes 11 recommendations:

- immediate action in hotspots where there is blatant racism;
- given the interlocking nature of racism and sexism, anti-discrimination structures should be created in the national Department of Education and provincial departments to monitor policy, and its implementation, towards all forms of discrimination;
- legislating so that all schools must develop an anti-discrimination policy and providing guidelines for such policies;
- anti-discrimination training involving an anti-racist approach for district officials, governing bodies, teachers and students;

- anti-racist training as an integral part of in-service and pre-service teacher training;
- the need for school clustering to increase involvement of black parents and racial mixing of learners;
- the need to place social justice values more firmly at the heart of the new outcomes-based curriculum (see chapter 3);
- examining ways of eliminating the gap between policy and implementation;
- the need to take a whole school development approach to anti-racism;
- designating a special day to focus on anti-discrimination; and
- utilising art and culture to assist anti-discriminatory procedures.

The report admits that it did not have time to flesh out these proposals and no consideration is given, for example, to funding or who will do the training and facilitate change. However, as it also says, its main role was 'to bring these matters to the public consciousness' so that methods of dealing with the problem can be devised. It certainly brings home the magnitude of the task involved given that all students will go on to become South African citizens, and therefore anti-discrimination training must be part of the education of all students whether they be in a recently desegregated school or a racially or ethnically homogeneous school.

A Case Study

An example of the more positive direction that desegregated schools could take is provided by a girls' school in Durban which I studied during the 1996 school year. This is described briefly here and in more detail in Harber (1998) and Welgemoed (1998). Until 1991, the school was all white by law but by 1996, the student population had become 60% white and 40% black – Indian, coloured and African in South African terms. The change in the racial composition of the school was difficult for staff and students brought up under apartheid. In 1994, students were asked to write about their feelings towards the school and the following are some examples of the responses:

There were times when I got back home crying, not only because of the pain I had endured from racial tension but also from the pain of seeing how much hatred young people can have in them. Because of the colour of my skin I am expected to fight and sweat for what I want. All I want is to be treated equally.

I wish things could be the way they were before they came to our school.

There will always be some whites that pretend to respect you because you're black. They think we Africans are stupid and do not see their deceitful smiles. We do not need their pity. I always see when they pretend and I just pretend I do not notice.

The blacks do not have any self-discipline.

Increasingly aware of the need for actively initiating change, in the 1995 edition of the school magazine the principal made an explicit link between non-racism and democratic values:

The most significant set of new challenges which has accompanied our growth is our development as a large multicultural school for girls in a new democratic South Africa. Having girls of different culture, religion, race, language and skin colour in a school does not necessarily make it multicultural. A school which is truly multicultural is one in which each pupil is valued equally by other pupils and by staff alike; one in which all pupils display mutual respect and make every effort to understand each person's language and culture; to respect their choice of religion; their right to voice their opinions and to accept each person's individuality. A truly multicultural school is one in which the pupils and staff are free from any form of discrimination or prejudice.

In late 1995 and during 1996, with the help of a consultant in the management of change, the principal began a process of school democratisation which pre-empted the South African Schools Act by introducing an elected school council, two members of which were also members of the school's governing body. However, democratic skills and values are learned, not inborn or developed by chance. Therefore, all class representatives underwent a training session which included a clear description of their role and focused on such skills as communicating effectively, handling conflict, managing a group and applying a democratic style of leadership in the classroom.

Moreover, the school embarked on a process of drafting a new key document which embodied a statement of shared values and behaviours, a new code of conduct and school rules and a new set of disciplinary procedures. Staff, students and parents were divided up into 28 workshops in which the new political context for South African education was discussed along with the need for a new, agreed set of basic values and rules to fully reflect the new context. The resulting 'behaviours for living our core values' included: 'be open-minded; respect others' values and beliefs; be willing to learn, adapt and mix, developing friends from different cultures; treat others as equals; resolve conflict constructively and express yourself honestly but tactfully'.

Interviews were held with both students and staff to assess their perceptions of the impact of the changes. The students were adamant that there was much less tension and frustration in the school because good two-way communication had been established. As a result, there was much less trouble in the school and almost no physical or verbal violence. One of the black members of the student representative council specifically stressed that there had been a dramatic decrease in the racist comments which she and others had experienced in the past. She attributed this to the overt and continually stressed commitment to mutual respect which was a key democratic value underlying the changes and the emphasis placed on equality whereby everybody gets a say. Students also commented on the mixed race nature of the change committee which had been established to oversee the process of change and that the upfront attitude to combating racism had helped. The staff interviewed noted the existence of racial tensions and conflicts in the school prior to the changes. They said that the changes had brought about much greater awareness of racial and multicultural issues as a result of the clear school policy that had been adopted, and that racial issues were dealt with openly and directly in a climate of increased communication and understanding.

Language

Language issues were central to the struggle against apartheid. It was the attempt to impose Afrikaans, perceived as the language of the oppressor, as the medium of instruction in black schools that sparked the Soweto uprisings of 1976. The South African Constitution, formally adopted in 1996, did not establish a national language but instead recognised 11 official languages – Sepedi, Sosotho, Setswana, siSwati, Tshivenda, Xitsonga, Afrikaans, English, isiNdebele, isiXhosa and isiZulu. This is in marked contrast to neighbouring Namibia where, despite a linguistic history of African languages, German and Afrikaans, English was adopted as the national language at independence in 1990 because of its international status and its widespread use in southern African countries. In practice, through its official use and use in the media, English is fast becoming the lingua franca in South Africa.

In terms of education, section 29(2) of the South African Constitution states that:

> *Everyone has the right to receive education in the official language or languages of their choice in public educational institutions where that education is reasonably practicable. In order to ensure the effective access to, and implementation of, this right, the state must consider all reasonable educational alternatives, including single medium institutions, taking into account:*

  – *equity*
  – *practicability and*
  – *the need to redress the results of past racially discriminatory*
    laws and practices.

Two key points need to be noted. The first is the inclusion of the phrase 'reasonably practicable'. This means that language rights in education are qualified or socially contextual rights, not absolute rights. The second is the inclusion of the possibility of single-medium schools – the state cannot therefore insist on more than one language of learning being provided by a school. As Brown (1998) notes, this position was argued for largely by Afrikaans interest groups. Afrikaans is the only language, other than English, which provides a language of learning throughout the education system. African languages are available as languages of learning only for the first few years of primary school.

    Under the 1996 South African Schools Act, school governing bodies, in conjunction with provincial and national levels of government, now have the power to choose the language(s) of learning (medium[s] of instruction) and the languages available as subjects at their schools. Moreover, the Department of Education's 1997 policy document *Norms and Standards Regarding Language Policy in Education* espouses an official policy of 'additive multilingualism' and 'additive bilingualism' which aims at a well-developed educational competence in two or more languages rather than taking language learning to partial levels only. This could lead to some difficult and complex choices. Brown (1998) cites the following example:

> *Matatiele Primary School in KwaZulu Natal is an ex-Griqua community school, which was a single-medium Afrikaans school. Subsequently, it changed to a parallel/dual medium school offering English and Afrikaans as the two languages of learning and is currently phasing out Afrikaans. The school offers two languages as subjects, English (first and second language) and Afrikaans (first and second language). However, the social and linguistic profile of its pupils has changed dramatically in the last three years, with 55% now speaking either Sesotho or isiXhosa in almost equal numbers. Neither of the two indigenous languages is dominant in the province of KwaZulu Natal where isiZulu predominates but both are prevalent in the Matatiele/Kokstad district.*

Which medium(s) of instruction will the school choose? Which indigenous language will be taught as a subject as many children come from homes which are bilingual in both? If it offered both, it would be committing itself to providing four languages at a time when none of the teachers is formally trained in isiXhosa or Sesotho. As Brown points out, it cannot be assumed that parents will request the provision of even one indigenous language and they may not necessarily be aware of their rights or want to exercise them.

However, despite the official policy of additive bilingualism and despite international evidence on the cognitive benefits and learning achievement advantages of such bilingual approaches (Martin, 1997), it seems that both the Constitution and resource issues have created a situation where in practice the majority of schools have opted for a single-medium, use of English approach. Researchers from the President's Education Initiative found that the majority of governing bodies have not developed formal language policies in line with legislation. Schools have also not changed their language policies even when there is a change in the language profile of the pupils. Often the staff's language proficiency and parental preference for high status languages (e.g. English) determine the language policy in a school.

In the study of 90 desegregated schools carried out by the South African Human Rights Commission, English was the language of instruction and learning in 31 schools and Afrikaans in 30 schools, with 17 schools parallel medium and 2 dual medium in all grades (that is where educators use both languages simultaneously to cater for learners of both languages in one classroom). None of the schools offered an indigenous language as a language of instruction and learning. None of the schools in Northern Cape, Eastern Cape or Mpumalanga offered languages other than English or Afrikaans as subjects and in the other provinces only a small minority did so. The authors conclude that:

> *Most schools are not moving proactively toward multilingualism and do not see language diversity as a school and classroom resource but rather as a deficiency ... there exists little acknowledgement or indication that perhaps educators and learners should learn an African language ... educators by and large fail to grasp the principles of additive bilingualism (that) it is essential to be fluent in one's first language in order to learn a second language effectively ... The result of neglecting or undermining the home language of learners is that learners are not able to develop their cognitive and academic skills sufficiently either in their home language or in a second language. (Vally & Dalamba, 1999, pp. 44–45)*

Gender

The South African Constitution is based on a philosophy of democracy and human rights and makes it very clear that discrimination on the basis of gender is unacceptable. Yet a woman is raped in South Africa every 90 seconds. Relying on the police for help and protection can be problematic – a recent study by the Institute for Security Studies revealed that a policeman rapes a woman every 2½ days (*Guardian*, 8 September 1999). Another survey revealed that one in three Johannesburg schoolgirls have been raped or sexually assaulted but that just 12% knew that it was illegal. In the same survey, more than one in ten schoolboys admitted to having raped or sexually assaulted a girl. Nearly half said they believe a girl means yes when she says no, while 16% believe girls enjoy being raped and almost one-third said the victims 'ask for it' (McGreal, 1999).

In October 1997, the report of the Gender Equity Task Team on gender equity in education was published (Wolpe et al, 1997). This 290-page document provides both an authoritative and comprehensive account of the present state of affairs with regard to gender issues in South African education and a series of policy proposals to tackle sexism, sexual harassment and sexual violence in the education system. The main conclusion of the report is unequivocal. On the back cover it states that 'South African education is riddled with gender inequities that impact negatively on girls and boys, women and men – but especially on the quality of life and achievements of women'. The following are some quotations from the document:

> *On one occasion members of the Task Team were told how men attending the workshop would return to their homes at night and insist that their wives crawl on the floor with their husbands' supper held in their hands. (p. 24)*

> *At a meeting of people involved in early childhood development a headmistress recounted how she was given pocket money by her husband, even though she contributed significantly to the household income. (p. 24)*

> *Another Task Team member described a practice that she said was not uncommon in schools, by teachers and more generally. She said it was usual for men to 'touch the titties of girls', then put their hands up their skirts, touch their genitalia and sniff their fingers. She was righteously indignant. Although not chronicled, this was accepted practice by boys and men, and was perhaps tolerated by girls who did not know how else to handle it. (p. 51)*

> *Unpublished qualitative research on the experiences of 150 African women teachers … revealed that their current experiences replicated their experiences as learners. They said that as schoolgirls they were not expected to think critically. Now they leave all decision making to male colleagues, even when men are in the minority. The women found that when they made points during meetings they were ignored while the*

same issues, if made by men, were accepted ... Female
secondary school teachers also highlighted the problem of
sexual harassment by fellow teachers as well as mature male
learners. These practices were often implicitly sanctioned by
school leaders and seldom led to any intervention or sanction
of the offender. (p. 83)

It is clear from these statements and from the document in general that historically, gender issues have tended to take second place to issues surrounding race and ethnicity in the struggle against apartheid. The report notes that it is only very recently that work on gender and education has been undertaken in South Africa and regrets the lack of networks in this area, necessitating the use of three visiting consultants from the United Kingdom and Australia. The lengthy and detailed nature of the report means that it is impossible to provide a full discussion of the recommendations and arguments of this important document here. However, a selection of key statements follows in order to at least give a flavour of the some of the main findings, ideas and recommendations of the report and the depth of change required.

There need to be classroom discussions, innovations in the
curriculum, monitoring of all forms of violence against girls
and women in educational institutions and disciplinary
procedures in place and operative whether it is a teacher or
student who is responsible for an act of violence.

The provinces are at different levels of development. They
have few formal structures to promote gender equity, a lack of
clarity in the main on what their briefs should be in this regard
and no allocated resources to tackle the matter.

Children as young as 2 and 3 have developed prejudicial
attitudes, as research has shown. Because the formative years
of early learning are crucial in developing non-racist and non-
sexist attitudes, the curriculum in early childhood
development needs to address these issues practically.

To effect change, educators themselves will need to have
meaningful and in-depth training ... These people, and others,
who may well be unaware of their own prejudices, will need to
engage in work that leads them to recognise their forms of
behaviour and how it impacts negatively on their charges. In-
service training of a specific nature will need to be devised for
current teachers and the curriculum for student teachers will
have to be drastically revised.

> *There are a number of structural constraints in higher education that militate against women's progress and development for both staff and students. These relate to parental leave, childcare facilities, and behavioural and ideological factors among other things. Women staff, for example, may be discriminated against in the course of appointments, promotions and encouragement to conduct research. The ambience of institutions is non-supportive of women in covert ways. Behaviour in lecture halls may be threatening to women ... In some instances students have been known to be penalised for falling pregnant. Sexual harassment and violence, as in all other levels of education, are present in universities – and indeed in all higher education institutions – with rape being common on all campuses.*

> *Education management in South Africa has traditionally been and remains male dominated at the most senior levels of decision making. This requires a change in the nature of institutional culture and greater attention to gender equity in such matters as advertising, recruitment procedures, interviews, recognition of prior learning, promotion criteria, mentoring and appraisal.*

Very early in the report it states that:

> *Throughout the course of the Task Team's work, reference has been made to the need to include men and boys in any consideration of gender matters ... without the support and commitment of boys and men to a more equitable society in which girls and women are consistently disadvantaged or humiliated or harassed or suffer violence, little will change.*
> *(p. 2)*

Important here is the concept of 'hegemonic masculinity', which suggests that although a number of masculine identities coexist, there is a dominant version of masculinity which grants power and privilege to those who espouse and internalise it. Among its key characteristics are misogyny, homophobia, racism, compulsory heterosexuality, the importance of sport and the use or threat of violence (Morrell, 1998a). Violence in schools, an issue dealt with in some detail in chapter 4, was regarded by the Gender Equity Task Team as the major barrier to achieving gender equity in schools and there is no doubt about the importance of fostering alternative masculine identities in South Africa and elsewhere not predicated on the proving of manliness through various forms of martial activity, fighting and violence. It is also important to remember in this regard that, while the main victims of sexual violence are girls and women, the main victims of violence per se are boys and men.

One of the first ever workshops in South Africa on the subject of masculinity and schooling was held at the University of Natal, Durban in 1997 (Morrell, 1998b). This brought together international and local participants and discussed both the nature of masculinity in relation to education and initiatives that have been taken to work with boys and young men to reduce levels of violence. One local initiative is the work done by the Centre for the Study of Violence and Reconciliation in Johannesburg. The Youth Department of the CSVR was established in 1995 to concentrate on school-based education programmes, trauma management, teacher training and lobbying and advocacy work. It works with young males in high school on the challenges and problems that they face. Another component of their work is the Centre's Trauma Clinic, which, since 1991, has offered free counselling services to adults and children, some as young as 6 years of age, who have been the victims of violence. As well as operating on a curative level, the Clinic has also sought to reduce the incidence of violence through training and education with boys who have been both the perpetrators and victims of inappropriate sexual behaviour at school. A second example of a local initiative is ADAPT (Agisanang Domestic Abuse and Prevention), which is based in Alexandra and which works with young men in the townships who have been involved in violent relationships, as well as with young men in schools. Their starting point is to develop responsibility in those who have been violent and to develop a climate of openness and support to permit young men to confront and overcome the need to affirm their masculinity through violence. The approach often promotes cathartic personal recognition and draws observers into disclosive encounters with other members of the group. Such work by non-governmental organisations not only points to the way ahead for schools themselves in regard to gender but also to the type of school environment required to combat discrimination in general. As Morrell (1998b, p. 223) puts it:

> *For gender justice to be promoted in education requires not*
> *just the protection of victims of violence nor the prosecution of*
> *the perpetrators of violence. It requires, rather, a wholesale*
> *transformation of school environments such that tolerance,*
> *respect and democratic-decision-making become the norm.*
> *For this to occur, the entire fabric of power relations (and the*
> *prejudices and discriminations which attest thereto) in school*
> *has to be worked with. A key part of any programme to create*
> *such an environment has to be engagement with hegemonic*
> *masculinity and the allowance for alternative masculinities to*
> *develop.*

Conclusion

It is clear that repealing the legislation and dismantling the structures of apartheid is only the beginning. For South Africa to become the society envisaged in the Constitution there will have to be a major cultural change in terms of values and behaviours. The phrase 'the rainbow nation' may well have served a useful and positive political purpose in the early and mid-1990s but is now in danger of obscuring the very real problems of race, gender and other human rights issues which confront South African society and which have been discussed in this chapter. The education system can and must be a key agent in social transformation and an important aspect of this will be what is learnt in the classrooms and how such learning takes place. The following chapter therefore concerns the reform of curriculum and assessment.

CHAPTER 3

Qualifications, Curriculum and Assessment

The school that I attended epitomised the national authoritarian institutions. Firstly, the curriculum was devised by the government and the school carried this out. This curriculum was rigid and the learners would have no say in what they learnt ... The teacher was the centre of the process and the learners were just passive ... All knowledge that was learnt was for the purpose of exams which were the only form of assessment ... I am very harsh when criticising my school because of the fact that I fell to the submission and accepted everything obliviously. Only after I finished school did I realise how confined we were and I grew more in one year out of school than twelve years in school. (Postgraduate initial teacher education student, University of Natal)

Introduction

An immediate concern of the newly elected government in 1994 was curriculum reform. Under apartheid, the curriculum was based on the racist ideology of Christian National Education, which was constructed to discourage critical thought, enquiry and discussion and to encourage domination and submission. The first curriculum reform of the new government was therefore to remove racially offensive content from school syllabuses (Jansen, 1997). However, the major curriculum innovation since the end of apartheid has been the introduction of 'Curriculum 2005', a policy of changing teaching, learning and assessment to Outcomes Based Education (OBE), which began in the first year of primary and secondary school in 1998 and will be completed for all years by the year 2005. The new approach emphasises outcomes or competences in terms of what a learner will be able to do at the end of a learning process. The process of learning therefore becomes as important as the content of learning. OBE in schools is set in the wider context of the National Qualifications Framework (NQF), which is based on OBE principles and which establishes a national system that links all the different levels of education to each other. The language and structures of the NQF are quite complex but are essential to understanding curriculum reform in schools and this chapter therefore begins by discussing the wider NQF before discussing assessment and then focusing on the nature and implementation of OBE at the level of schools in particular.

The National Qualifications Framework

Interest in an NQF originated in the period 1989–94 when the Congress of South African Trade Unions, employers, educationalists, the ANC, members of the 'old' departments of education and labour and the Centre for Education Policy Development began to look at ways in which education and training could be improved. The NQF was based on a desire to integrate education and training in order to produce high quality and high skill human resources able to compete in the global economic market. The economic basis of the argument for an NQF was made in the 1995 *White Paper on Education and Training*:

> *Successful modern economies and societies require the elimination of artificial hierarchies, in social organisation, in the organisation and management of work, and in the way in which learning is organised and certified. They require citizens with a strong foundation of general education, the desire and ability to continue to learn, to adapt to and develop new knowledge, skills and technologies, to move flexibly between occupations, to take responsibility for personal performance, to set and achieve high standards and to work co-operatively. (Department of Education, 1995a, p. 15)*

The broad model of the NQF has been imported from a range of Western countries such as Australia, New Zealand and the United Kingdom, and reflects a desire to move away from a low trust, low ability society with bureaucratic and rigid forms of organisations:

> *The education system has therefore to shift from a system that differentiates and socialises students for the rigid hierarchical division of labour of modern industrial societies, to a system producing high ability – high quality products with the ability to solve problems, think critically and apply new skills and techniques to different situations. (de Clercq, 1997, p. 156)*

Through combining education and training, the NQF attempts to achieve a number of benefits. The first is in terms of coherence and portability, as the courses and qualifications offered in the different parts of the education and training systems did not link or articulate well with each other in the past. Making links between equivalent qualification levels explicit therefore allows mobility between, and progression across, different learning institutions and contexts. A second advantage is that it allows for the recognition of learning in informal settings through the accreditation of prior learning. Figure 1 sets out the basic structure of the NQF.

School Grades	NQF Level	Band	Types of Qualifications & Certificates	
	8	Higher Education and Training Band	Doctorates Further research degrees	
	7		Degrees, Diplomas and Certificates	
	6			
	5			
Further Education and Training Certificates				
12	4	Further Education and Training Band	School/College/NGOs Training Certificates, Mix of Units	
11	3		School/College/NGOs Training Certificates, Mix of Units	
10	2		School/College/NGOs Training Certificates, Mix of Units	
General Education and Training Certificates				
9 8	1	General Education and Training Band	Senior Phase	ABET 4
7 6 5			Intermediate Phase	ABET 3
4 3 2			Foundation Phase	ABET 2
1 R			Pre-school	ABET 1

Figure 1. Source: Department of Education (1997c).

The South African Qualifications Authority (SAQA) was established in 1995 to oversee the establishment and functioning of the NQF. It is governed by a board composed of representatives from different government departments, business, labour, providers of education and training, and important interest groups such as women, youth and the disabled. SAQA established National Standards Bodies (NSBs) to set agreed national standards for each designated area of knowledge at each level of the education system under their authority. Some NSBs, e.g. education, might only be involved in the higher education level whereas others, such as Communication and Languages, might cover the whole education and training system. Standard Generating Bodies (SGBs) are responsible for generating standards in particular fields and at particular levels. They ensure that practitioners are involved in setting standards in their own fields. In order to ensure that such standards are implemented, SAQA has established institutions called Education, Training and Quality Assurers (ETQAs) which have the responsibility to see that the providers of education and training prepare learners adequately to meet the new standards.

In line with OBE, 'standards' are interpreted under the NQF as the outcomes or resulting competences of education. Each competence is seen as having three dimensions:

- practical competence (the demonstrated ability to perform a set of tasks);
- foundational competence (the demonstrated understanding of what we are doing and why); and
- reflexive competence (the demonstrated ability to learn from our actions and adapt to changing circumstances).

McLean (1998, p. 43) provides a useful example of how this approach might apply to a qualification like teaching:

> *One way of developing the standards for a teaching qualification would be to ask what practical skills a teacher needs. These may include practical skills around designing lessons, finding and adapting materials, facilitating a class, assessing learners, and keeping records of progress of each learner. Each one of these might form a 'unit standard'. They could each be divided into more detailed descriptions of what a teacher should be able to do: for example, the practical skills for assessing learners might include designing an assessment task, administering the assessment, marking the assessment and giving feedback. These detailed descriptions of what somebody should be able to do are called 'performance outcomes' and each unit standard normally starts with a list of performance outcomes that a learner should be able to demonstrate before they are said to have achieved the*

standard. A standard at a lower level (for a beginner teacher) might include only a few performance outcomes; while a standard at a higher level (for an advanced teacher) might include more performance outcomes and/or more complex performance outcomes. The next step would be to ask what foundational competence somebody would need to do all these practical tasks effectively. For example, to facilitate a class a teacher might need to know how people learn, the subject she is teaching, and be able to communicate in the language of her learners. All these details would be written in the unit standard under a category called 'underpinning knowledge'. The next step would be to ask what a teacher would need to know and be able to do in order to achieve 'reflexive competence'. This might include some practical skills, such as keeping a journal with notes about her own teaching as well as some foundational skills such as knowing how to theorise her teaching, how to pose questions and find answers to those questions and how to use the library to do further reading about the issues.

Outcomes Based Education and Schools

To take OBE to its logical conclusion one would not need traditional school subjects at all as what matters are the desired outcomes, competences or performances, and subject content (*what* is taught) would be irrelevant as long as the outcomes were achieved. Indeed, assessment in the secondary schools community extension project in Papua New Guinea was based on a similar principle (Vulliamy, 1981). However, in South African schools, subjects have not been abolished but have been restructured as eight broad 'learning areas', thereby blurring and softening the boundaries between subjects a little rather than abandoning them altogether. The eight learning areas are Communication, Literacy and Language Learning; Numeracy and Mathematics; Human and Social Science; Natural Sciences; Arts and Culture; Economic and Management Sciences; Life Orientation; and Technology.

The Department of Education has contrasted the main differences between what it sees as the old approaches to curriculum and the new OBE approach (see Table I).

Differences between 'old' and 'new' approaches	
Old	New
passive learners	active learners
exam-driven	learners are assessed on an on-going basis
rote-learning	critical thinking, reasoning, reflection and action
syllabus is content-based and broken down into subjects	an integration of knowledge; learning relevant and connected to real-life situations
textbook/worksheet bound and teacher centred	learner-centred; teacher is facilitator; teacher constantly uses groupwork and teamwork to consolidate the new approach
sees syllabus as rigid and non-negotiable	learning programmes seen as guides that allow teachers to be innovative and creative in designing programmes
teachers responsible for learning; motivation dependent on the personality of the teacher	learners take responsibility for their learning; pupils motivated by constant feedback and affirmation of their worth
emphasis on what the teacher hopes to achieve	emphasis on outcomes – what the learner becomes and understands
content placed into rigid time-frames	flexible time-frames allow learners to work at their own pace
curriculum development process not open to public comment	comment and input from the wider community is encouraged

Table I. Source: Department of Education, 1997b, pp. 6–7.

SAQA have designed eight 'critical cross-field' or essential outcomes that apply to all levels of education. These are that learners should be able to successfully demonstrate their ability to do the following.

- Communicate effectively using visual, mathematical and/or language skills in the modes of oral and/or written presentation.
- Identify and solve problems by using creative and critical thinking.
- Organise and manage themselves and their activities responsibly and effectively.
- Work effectively with others in a team, group, organisation and community.
- Collect, analyse, organise and critically evaluate information.
- Use science and technology effectively and critically, showing responsibility towards the environment and the health of others.

- Understand that the world is a set of related systems. This means that problem-solving contexts do not exist in isolation.
- Show awareness of the importance of effective learning strategies, responsible citizenship, cultural sensitivity, education and career opportunities and entrepreneurial abilities. (Department of Education, 1997b)

There are also some 66 specific learning outcomes related to the particular learning areas. Examples from the Languages, Literacy and Communication learning area would be 'Learners show critical awareness of language usage', 'Learners respond to the aesthetic, affective, cultural and social values in texts' and 'Learners access, process and use information from a variety of sources and situations' (Department of Education, 1997b). As the outcomes cited earlier demonstrate, competences tend to be defined quite broadly in terms of generic skills and knowledge, and not in a very narrow, behaviourist manner. In fact, in South Africa they have been described as 'transformational competences', precisely to distinguish them from technical checklists of skills. Also, despite the origins of NQF in debate about the economy, it is clear that the Government intended outcomes to apply to a wide range of learning experiences not directly or solely related to employment and the economy, including, for example, human rights, multilingualism and multiculturalism.

Assessment

The first common, non-racial senior certificate (school leaving) examination for all South Africans was introduced in 1996. While this is good news, the bad news is that it was still a traditional form of examination and there has been much soul searching about why pass rates have tended to decline since. Here, however, the concern is more with the processes of assessment, because if OBE is to succeed, then school assessment at all levels, including the senior certificate, will need to be reformed. Teachers (and pupils) often start with what is to be assessed and work backwards – the so-called backwash effect. So, if there is to be a move from a content-based and teacher-centred curriculum to an outcomes based curriculum, then methods of assessment in South Africa must move away from overreliance on the traditional timed examination based on memorisation. The general intention to change in the direction of continuous assessment was made clear when the Government launched its Curriculum 2005 in February 1997:

> *Assessment will be on-going. That means a learner's progress*
> *will be monitored continuously ... A variety of assessment*
> *methods will be available to ensure that the methods are*
> *suited to the performance being assessed ... Evidence*
> *collection for use in assessment will be on-going, linked with*

> the normal course of learning or working and not from one-off
> assessment occasions ... The methods used will be
> straightforward, pre-arranged and will not interfere unduly
> with learning. (Department of Education, 1997b, p. 19)

Certainly, assessment criteria for the eight learning areas were produced
at the same time and duly divided into senior phase, intermediate phase
and foundation phase according to the NQF. Each phase is accompanied
by a 'range statement', that is, an indication of the scope, depth, level of
complexity and parameters of achievement. They include indications of
the critical areas of content, processes and context which the learner
should engage with in order to reach an acceptable level of achievement.
Figure 2 is from a discussion document published in March 1997 and
sets out specific outcomes, assessment criteria and range statements for
all eight learning areas from grades 1 to 9. The document is 237 pages
long. The example concerns the specific outcome 'Learners respond to
the aesthetic, affective, cultural and social values in texts'.

3: Learners respond to the aesthetic, affective, cultural and social values in texts			
The aim of this outcome is to develop a learner's appreciation, use and creation of text as an artistic expression of thoughts, feelings, attitudes and values through exposure to a wide variety of genres. The development of learners' listening, reading and viewing skills to recognise and use literary devices enriches the quality of their own language use and lives.			
Phase		Assessment criteria	Range statement
S	1	Responses to the artistic effects of texts are demonstrated	At this level, learners engage with a wide variety of texts in a variety of contexts.
	2	Literary effects of texts are identified, analysed and described	The emphasis in terms of content is on: – the expression of stylistic devices (e.g. extended metaphor) in all kinds of texts
	3	Opinions on texts are given and justified	– the study of literary, visual, auditory and multi-media texts.
	4	Opinions are reviewed in relation to the opinions of others	The emphasis in terms of process is on the enriching effect of texts in
	5	Texts are critically evaluated	relation to: – knowledge (e.g. related to history, social conditions, human

	6	Response to text is linked to personal life and the lives of others	social conditions, human experiences, human rights) – aesthetics (e.g. appreciation of the artistic elements) – relationships (e.g. social sensibility, power relations) – emotions (e.g. sympathy, empathy, identification, rejection)
I	1	Responses to the artistic effects of texts are demonstrated	At this level, learners engage with a range of appropriate texts in different contexts. The emphasis is on: – the expression of stylistic devices (e.g. personification, onomatopoeia) in all kinds of texts – responding to literary, visual, auditory and multi-media texts The emphasis in terms of process is on the enriching effect of texts in relation to: – emotions (e.g. sympathy, empathy, identification, rejection) – knowledge (e.g. related to history, social conditions, human experiences, human rights) – relationships (e.g. social sensibility, power relations) – aesthetics (e.g. appreciation of the artistic elements)
	2	Literary effects of texts are recognised and described	
	3	Response to text is linked to personal life and the lives of others	
	4	Opinions on texts are given and justified	
	5	Opinions are reviewed in relation to the opinions of others	
	6	Texts are critically evaluated	
F	1	Responses to the artistic effects of texts are demonstrated	At this level, learners engage with a range of appropriate texts in different contexts. The emphasis is on: – the expression of stylistic devices (e.g. rhyme, repetition, alliteration) in all kinds of texts – responding to literary, visual, auditory and multi-media texts The emphasis in terms of process is on the enriching effect of texts in relation to:
	2	Literary effects of texts are recognised	
	3	Response to text is linked to personal life	
	4	Opinions on texts are given	
	5	Opinions are reviewed in relation to the opinions of others	

	6	Texts are critically evaluated	– emotions (e.g. sympathy, empathy, identification, rejection) – knowledge (e.g. related to history, social conditions, human experiences, human rights) – relationships (e.g. social sensibility, power relations) – aesthetics (e.g. appreciation of the artistic elements)

Figure 2. Source: Department of Education, 1997c.

Surprisingly, however, given the backwash effect, a new pupil assessment policy was only announced in November 1998, well into the first year of implementation of OBE, and was only to come into effect in 1999, the second year of implementation. This lack of synchronisation echoes one of the criticisms of OBE that will be discussed further below. In this new policy, continuous assessment using a diverse range of techniques (written tests, oral questions and answers, interviewing, self-assessment, peer assessment, portfolios, observation sheets, journals, projects and written assignments) was seen as the best model for assessing OBE. Internal assessment with external moderation would be the normal practice except at Grade 9 (the end of secondary school) when assessment would be designed, planned, administered and moderated by an examining body. Expected levels of performance for each grade and phase were to be developed, which each learner would be required to meet in order to be promoted from one grade to the next, though the purpose was partly diagnostic so that pupils would be helped to develop during the year and no pupil should spend more than 4 years in each of the three phases of schooling. An amount of R1.2 billion has been set aside from the Policy Reserve Fund for the training of teachers in the new forms of assessment (Department of Education, 1998b; Motala, 1998).

'Ten Reasons Why OBE will Fail'

However, OBE is not without its critics. In an important paper, Jansen (1998) puts forward 10 major reasons why he thinks OBE will have a negative impact upon South African schools. He argues that OBE will fail not because politicians and bureaucrats are misinformed about the conditions of South African schooling but because the policy was being driven in the first instance by political imperatives which have little to do with the realities of classroom life. His first objection, and one that may be shared with readers who have got to this point in the chapter, is that the language of innovation associated with OBE and the NQF is too complex, confusing and inaccessible for South African teachers. A teacher trying to come to terms with OBE has to understand over 50 different concepts (competences, outcomes, unit standards, equivalence, articulation, assessment criteria, range statements, bands, levels, phases and their relationship to SAQA, the NQF, NSBs, SGBs and ETQAs). Jansen, who is a Professor of Education at the University of Durban-Westville comments that 'I still find the maze of jargon and tortured definitions intimidating', a view shared by this ex-Professor of Education at a neighbouring university.

Jansen's second argument is that OBE is too closely associated with helping economic growth while there is little international evidence of a close causal link between education and economic prosperity. While this is one of the reasons for the introduction of OBE, and the lack of clear evidence of any such direct relationship is true, there is nevertheless evidence from government publications and from the specified outcomes that it is about more than economic growth. He also argues, as we have seen from the contrast between 'old' and 'new' (Table I), that OBE policy drastically overstates the pedagogical changes that are likely to take place in the classroom as the claims that it makes 'represent a conceptual leap of staggering proportions from outcomes to dramatic changes in the social relations in the classroom'. The reason why a dramatic change to these methods is unlikely is Jansen's third criticism – that existing conditions in schools will not allow for such changes. To be successful the policy would require a critical mass of highly qualified, professional and committed teachers, something which the next two chapters of this book suggests is not yet the case in South Africa. Without sufficient cadres of such teachers, Jansen argues, OBE will either not happen or, despite the enlightened model of transformational competences, will actually be interpreted narrowly in accordance with a more mechanical model of behaviourism.

His fourth criticism is a philosophical questioning of the compatibility of specifying outcomes in advance with a democratic school system. There is, he argues, a fundamental contradiction between insisting that students use knowledge creatively only to inform them that the desired learning outcomes are already specified. This is connected to his fifth problem with OBE, which is that, in contrast to the history of the ANC during the educational and political struggle of the 1980s when the processes of learning were valued in themselves, the introduction of OBE was not really a curriculum change process in which teachers were fully involved. Instead, it was imposed and teachers are defined as implementers while official support has been uneven, fragmented and for many teachers non-existent. His sixth criticism is that OBE enables policy-makers to avoid values and therefore asking the central question of what education in South Africa is for. He argues that the learning outcomes are too bland and decontextualised and as a result could be interpreted very differently in different contexts. 'Good citizenship', for example, could mean very different things in a conservative school setting to that of a school with a democratic ethos. However, while this may be true of the way the Curriculum 2005 outcomes have been written, it is not the case that the overall values, purpose and aims of education in post-apartheid South Africa are unclear. All schools, for example, should have a democratic ethos and schools and teachers are expected to interpret OBE in the light of broader policy and legislation. What is problematic is whether teachers are aware of policies in the first place or agree with them and this will be discussed in chapter 5.

Jansen's seventh criticism is that OBE will multiply the administrative burden on teachers, particularly via the record keeping and other demands of continuous assessment in a context where average class sizes are set to increase. His eighth point is that OBE trivialises curriculum content when content matters. For example, 'appreciating the richness of national and cultural heritages' could be based on content which glorifies a narrow Afrikaner nationalism or a militant ethnic Africanism and this could damage attempts to build a multicultural curriculum that engages with such matters in the historical context of apartheid South Africa. OBE also assumes that knowledge acquisition proceeds in a linear fashion so that one outcome is linked to the next in a steplike manner, which is highly questionable but has been ignored in the move towards implementation.

His ninth criticism is that if OBE is to succeed even moderately, then a whole raft of other innovations must come into play at the same time, such as retrained teachers, new forms of assessment, different classroom teaching methods, new systems of monitoring and evaluation, retrained principals and educational administrators and new learning resources. Yet: 'There is neither the fiscal base nor the political will to intervene in the education system at this level of intensity'. Jansen's tenth and final point concerns assessment. He argues that there is international evidence that suggests that assessment techniques do not change radically despite the introduction of OBE. He argues that hurried discussions in the Learning Area Committees in South Africa were not in fact accompanied by intensive debates about the reorganisation of the assessment system and that as a result traditional examinations will continue to play a powerful role in shaping teaching and learning.

Not a single official in the Ministry of Education interviewed by Jansen believed that OBE should be introduced as early as 1998, yet they all worked feverishly to get it implemented then at all costs. Overall, he concludes by arguing that OBE should be seen as an act of political symbolism in which the primary preoccupation of the state is with its own legitimacy, particularly in terms of a political need for the Ministry of Education to be seen to be doing something towards school transformation.

Outcomes Based Education in Practice

Are these doubts and criticisms valid? What has happened to this major attempt at curriculum innovation so far? In terms of the process of implementation, there is no doubt that throughout 1996 and 1997, as the policy was being developed, there were regular complaints of lack of consultation and insufficient time to prepare and retrain. The South African Democratic Teachers Union, for example, said that the process was being driven by the bureaucracy and there should be greater involvement of teachers and students and more time before it was introduced (Kgobe, 1996). Professor Danie Schreuder of Stellenbosch described the lack of teacher involvement as a flaw: 'Without teacher involvement it's like the top management of a car manufacturing company designing a new model in the boardroom while on the factory floor workers are still manufacturing a 1954 model' (*The Teacher*, January 1997). One interesting indicator of the haste of implementation was that a national pilot and training scheme was planned for the second half of 1997 – after the official launch of the new curriculum in February/March. As one observer put it:

> *Of course a different and better conceived course of action would have seen the pilot and training take place before the learning areas and outcomes were identified and finalised. This would have allowed the experience of teachers and learners to be drawn more directly into the process and enabled officials to plan in a more informed manner. As it now stands, the framework has been designed in isolation from the concrete context of teaching, learning and training, under state-driven rather than education-driven imperatives.* (Greenstein, 1997, p. 6)

OBE officially commenced in grades 1 and 7 in January 1998. At the end of the first school term in 1998, provincial reports indicated that up to half of the primary schools in some provinces had ignored the launch of Curriculum 2005. Pilot evaluations of grade 1 classrooms in several provinces had shown the differential impact of the new curriculum policy on poor as opposed to well-resourced schools. A study of 39 schools in KwaZulu Natal revealed that:

- most black schools had not started implementing Curriculum 2005;
- most white schools believe they have been doing OBE anyway and do not need to change anything; and
- white teachers had accumulated resources and support materials well beyond the short informational sessions provided by the provincial department of education, while black teachers had very few support materials.

In rural areas, it was estimated that at least 20,000 primary schools had failed to implement the new curriculum for reasons such as lack of teacher preparation or lack of resource materials. Conversely, in many of the former model C schools, teachers have resisted attending workshops or implementing Curriculum 2005 and dismiss it as 'simplistic', 'repetitive' and 'watering down standards'. Across the country, most teachers expressed similar views about lack of information, resources or teaching materials for implementing the new curriculum. Teachers that had already begun to implement the new curriculum had begun to realise that there are particular practices required to make OBE work. Some teachers raised concerns about organising group work and integrating content with little time set aside during the school day for lesson planning or collaborating with other colleagues. Others raised concerns about how the school calendar and the school day will be structured if learning and assessment are individualised and done on an as-needed basis. However, despite the concerns raised, most teachers still expressed enthusiasm and hope for the vision set out by Curriculum 2005. The general perception was that it will provide new ways of achieving equity and redress (Vally & Spreen, 1998).

Similarly, a report on research carried out by the Presidential Education Initiative published in 1999 indicated that OBE is succeeding in the ideological domain, with teachers embracing its main intentions. However, many teachers did not have the conceptual resources to give effect to it in the classrooms. Teachers, particularly in poorly resourced schools, were not in a position to translate the broad outcomes of Curriculum 2005 into appropriate learning programmes nor to develop their own assessment strategies. Some researchers observed significant contradictions between teachers' verbal support of the learner-centred pedagogy of Curriculum 2005 and the actual practices of these same teachers. The following practices were commonly observed:

- teacher talk and low-level questions dominate lessons;
- lessons are generally characterised by a lack of structure and the absence of activities which promote higher order skills such as investigation, understanding relationships and curiosity;
- real world examples are often used but at a very superficial level;
- little group work or other interaction occurs between pupils;
- pupils do little reading or writing; when it exists, it is often of a very rudimentary kind.

The report of the Presidential Education Initiative stressed the importance of pre- and in-service education programmes in helping teachers to develop sound conceptual frameworks related to OBE (Vally, 1999).

Local studies of the implementation of OBE in schools have also been carried out by students doing dissertations for their higher degrees.

One example (Russell, 1998) of a study of the introduction of OBE into three primary schools in Durban again found that teachers were positive about OBE and felt that the children were generally benefiting from the change. The teachers were beginning to alter their classroom practice but they also identified a range of important problems such as the top–down nature of the reform and the confusing speed of change, using an outcomes-based approach with large classes of over 40 children and the increased administration caused by the routine of recording marks for continuous assessment.

Conclusion

That all has not gone perfectly and smoothly in the planning and implementation of Curriculum 2005 has been implicitly recognised by the Minister of Education, who in February 2000 established a Review Committee to be chaired by Professor Linda Chisholm of the University of Natal. In June 2000, the Committee concluded that, while there was overwhelming support for outcomes-based education, Curriculum 2005 was too complex and confusing for most teachers to use and that implementation had been hampered by inadequate teacher training, lack of good quality support materials, policy overload and shortages of staff and resources. The Committee recommended a reduction in the number of learning areas from eight to six, scrapping the 66 specific outcomes (but retaining the critical outcomes) and also simplifying other complex assessment and performance measures (MacGregor, 2000b).

Teachers will obviously be vital to the eventual success or failure of these reforms. One set of commentators on this speech (Motala et al, 1999) made an important point when they argued that a balance will have to be struck between providing support materials to teachers and enabling them to be critical, independent curriculum developers. While teachers need help, externally prepared support materials tend to deskill teachers and deny them the opportunity to be creative and become empowered through being involved in the intellectual work of developing alternatives in the teaching and learning process. Indeed, part of the rationale behind Curriculum 2005 was that it would allow for contextual interpretation by teachers in the diverse school environments of South Africa. However, the other side of the same coin is the finding of the 1994 National Teacher Education Audit that the majority of South African teachers have not been prepared in their teacher education to make curricular decisions, so it will be difficult for them to meet the Minister's expectations. There is a close connection between curriculum development and implementation and teacher education. Similarly, the way that teachers see themselves and their work will also affect curriculum and other reforms in practice. Chapter 5 therefore examines the nature of teacher education and teacher identity in South Africa.

However, before this, it is also important to understand in more detail the conditions in which teachers in South Africa work and the school contexts into which the curriculum reform has been introduced. This is the theme of chapter 4.

CHAPTER 4

Life in Schools: the culture of learning and teaching

Introduction

The implementation of management and curriculum reform in South African schools will mean changing the ways schools operate. At the moment, the 'culture of learning, teaching and service' is often identified as a barrier or obstacle to such change. The following, for example, is an extract from a speech made by the Deputy Minister of Education in 1997 at a conference about the Culture of Learning, Teaching and Service Campaign, which will be further discussed below. Few role players in education escape scathing criticism:

> *In many of our education departmental offices, there is a chronic absenteeism of officials, appointments are not honoured, punctuality is not observed, phones ring without being answered, files and documents are lost, letters are not responded to, senior officials are inaccessible, there is confusion about roles and responsibilities and very little support, advice and assistance is given to schools ... Many of our parents fear their own children, never check the child's attendance at school, are not interested in the welfare of the school, never attend meetings, give no support to the teacher or principal ... Many of our teachers are not committed to quality teaching, their behaviour leaves much to be desired, are more interested in their own welfare, are not professional and dedicated, are never at school on time, pursue their studies at the expense of the children, do not prepare for lessons ... Many of our children are always absent from school, lack discipline and manners, regularly leave school early, are usually late for school, wear no uniform, have no respect for teachers, drink during school hours, are involved in drugs and*

gangs, gamble and smoke at school, come to school armed to instil fear in others ... Many of our principals have no administrative skills, they are the source of conflict between students and teachers, sow divisions among their staff, undermine the development of their colleagues, fail to properly manage the resources of their school, do not involve parents in school matters. This has resulted in chaos, poor decisions, lack of imagination and a total collapse of the education system in many schools ... Many of our schools have no electricity, no water, no toilets, no libraries, no laboratories, no furniture, no classrooms, no teachers, no buildings, no windows, no pride and no dignity. (Mkhatshwa, 1997, pp. 14–15)

As this suggests, the physical conditions in schools, the values and behaviour of staff and students and the intrusion of violence from the wider society are not seen as conducive to an effective, safe and professional school environment in which genuine transformation can take place. This chapter discusses the nature of the culture of learning, teaching and service in South African schools, identifies good practice as well as problem areas and attempts to analyse why such problems exist.

Resources

There are enormous disparities between schools in South Africa in terms of resource provision. While some schools can match the levels of resource provision in the schools of the industrialised north, there is no doubt that many schools are ill equipped to carry out an effective education. The *Schools Register of Needs Survey* revealed that one-quarter of all schools in South Africa do not have water available within walking distance and another 8% only have access to a communal tap. In KwaZulu Natal, for example, 2079 schools have electricity, 3311 do not. In South Africa as a whole, the majority of schools do not have electricity supplied or access to a telephone. In all provinces, there is a shortage of toilets for learners. Some 82% of schools in South Africa have no media equipment, two-thirds have no teaching equipment of any kind and textbook provision nationally is evenly divided between 'adequate' and 'inadequate'. In the majority of South African provinces over 40% of schools do not have any sports facilities and the majority of schools do not have a school typewriter or computer for administrative purposes. Nationally there is a shortage of 57,499 classrooms in which to teach the amount of learners enrolled in schools (Department of Education, 1997d). Even the obstacles faced in getting these data are indicative of the issues faced:

– *institutions which could only be reached on foot;*

– poor conditions of roads or lack of roads;

– an unexpectedly high rate of vehicle breakdowns, accidents, thefts and hijacking;

– difficulty in location of institutions due to incomplete lists or departmental staff not being available;

– some schools being uncooperative or staff members being absent. (Department of Education, 1997d, p. 4)

One conservative estimate argued that addressing the infrastructural requirements outlined in the *Schools Register of Needs Survey* would require R3 billion over a period of 10 years (Motala et al, 1999). Resources therefore continue to be a constraint on educational reform. One of the key priorities set out by Kadar Asmal, the new Minister of Education, when he took office after the 1999 general election was 'to end the physical degradation in South African schools'. A recent review of the current situation (Motala et al, 1999) noted, for example, that there continues to be a serious shortage of classrooms. There are, in fact, more educators than classrooms with the result that in some provinces only 70–80% of all educators can be fully utilised. The review also pointed out the significance of the increasing exercise of choice by parents. The perceived inability of the state to improve disadvantaged schools has resulted in many parents sending their children to former Model C schools. This has caused intakes in some disadvantaged schools to decrease by 40–60% a year. One result of a greater emphasis on choice and the market, therefore, is that financial resources in the form of fees and other contributions are going elsewhere – to already advantaged institutions.

Another issue highlighted by the review was the need to target resources more to meet specific conditions where the need is greatest. An example is the issue of farm schools in rural areas. The *Schools Register of Needs Survey* found that farm schools were amongst those having the greatest need. For example, by 1998, 88%, 56% and 100% of all schools without water, electricity and fencing respectively were farm schools. Farm schools have almost no essential teaching and learning resources. Diminishing farm worker populations have increased the number of relatively small farm schools. While small rural schools can have many educational advantages as well as disadvantages (Harber, 1996), there is no doubt that farm schools need a greater injection of resources. Post-1994 educational policy has not so far tackled the issue of funding for schools in rural areas nor has it addressed policies that might improve the quality of education for learners in these schools, such as those concerned with transport and clustering.

While national statistics are important in providing the overall picture, they obviously miss the complexity and uneven nature of the resource situation in particular schools. The following descriptions of two individual schools put some 'flesh and blood' on to the statistical bones. The first description comes from a Canadian visitor to a secondary school considered one of the better schools in a township outside Durban and the second forms part of a Centre for Education Policy Development research project and is of a farm school near Bloemfontein in the Free State.

From a distance the school looks abandoned. The four one-storey brick blocks built around a quadrangle display a forlorn patchwork of broken windows which the authorities no longer bother to repair. What was once a playground is now a dusty wasteland with goats grazing on the few remaining blades of grass. The school property is completely surrounded by a squatters' camp which sprung up in 1986 ... The first students we see as we approach are standard seven girls who are sweeping rubbish out of the classrooms (there are no maintenance staff) and into an alcove behind the staff toilet where it will be burnt. Burning rubbish has been an every-other-day event since the municipality stopped collecting rubbish from the school last year ... The facilities certainly aren't the school's main attraction. The library doesn't boast enough books for the students to take them out on loan. The science lab has just been equipped with portable plastic sink units which will eventually be connected to water and gas. When this happens the students will be able to conduct experiments for the first time. In the meantime the study of science remains completely theoretical. The computer lab currently houses 10 machines which are far from the state of the art and aren't connected to the Internet. Access to both the science and computer labs is restricted to a group of hand-picked students. It's the teachers who decide who will study these subjects and clearly they pick the brightest and the best. Typing, on the other hand, on the school's mostly manual machines, is open to everyone. (Fearnly, 1998)

The school consists of two relatively new buildings – one housing three classrooms and the other an ablution block. Two classrooms in the new building are separated by a folding door which, when opened, forms a small hall. According to parents, this hall is the pride of the local community and is the venue for numerous community and fund-raising activities. The classrooms are of an appropriate size for the 1:25 classroom/learner ratio. There are no specialist rooms

*and learners do not move from one classroom to another. All
subjects are taught in the same classroom. The school does not
have a library. The principal mentioned that she intends
reserving one cupboard in her classroom for library books that
were promised to the school by a local charity. The general
condition of the buildings is fairly good and this may be
attributed to the pride parents, educators and learners have in
their school. The school has neither an administration block
nor an office for the principal ... Although the schoolyard is
adequately fenced, the school buildings are without security
gates or security bars. Vandalism and theft is therefore a
problem. In addition, unused and decrepit buildings standing
in the schoolyard constitute a physical danger to learners and
may serve as a haven to vagrants. The school is without a
staffroom and educators frequently have their tea al fresco ...
The school has modern toilets in a fairly good condition ... The
classrooms are clean and neatly organised. There are many
charts on the wall, some of which are supplied by the
Department of Education ... Learners are seated at
combination bench-desks and there is adequate seating for all.
Educators have a chair and table. Overall, the furniture is in
good condition ... All three classrooms have chalkboards and
dusters. Since constructing the new building in 1995 the
school has had electricity and water is supplied by means of a
borehole. Parents pay R5 a month to cover the monthly
electricity account. Payment of the monthly premium is a
matter of contention with parents who feel that the electricity
bill should be borne by the Education Department.
Infrequently, water from the borehole is a terrible brown colour
and undrinkable. However, in the absence of drinking water
educators and learners have learnt to simply make do with
what they have. The school does not have a telephone and the
feeling of isolation and abandonment is enhanced by the lack
of communication with the Education Department. The school
is part of a nutrition-feeding scheme. It receives a daily supply
of bread and educators prepare sandwiches for the learners.
However, the delivery of the bread is often tardy and
unreliable. (Macpherson, 1998)*

The Culture of Learning, Teaching and Services

The Culture of Learning Programme was originally launched in July 1994
as part of the Reconstruction and Development Programme in order to
restore the culture of learning which had been badly damaged in many
parts of the country as a result of the constant disruption of education in

schools since 1976. The programme sought to reverse the absenteeism, indiscipline and destruction of school property generated by the conflict in educational institutions during the apartheid era. Subsequently relaunched as COLTS (the Culture of Learning, Teaching and Service campaign), it has been criticised for paying too much attention to the physical improvement of schools rather than acting directly on the *culture* of learning and teaching. While there is evidence that this emphasis on improving the physical infrastructure has helped to improve student attitudes and behaviour in Gauteng (Motala et al, 1999), there is nevertheless no doubt that much remains to be done in relation to the culture of learning and teaching. Another of Kadar Asmal's priorities on becoming Minister of Education in 1999, for example, was to 'develop the professional quality of our teaching force'.

This will not be an easy task. The following are a few newspaper headlines from recent years followed by a brief account of what appeared in the article concerned. Such articles appear in the press quite regularly.

> *'Crackdown on errant teachers': The KwaZulu Natal Minister of Education said that he was setting up a commission to probe teachers who were conducting private businesses from classrooms. These teachers were using cellphones to run illegal operations. Professor Jonathan Jansen of the University of Durban-Westville said he was also aware of teachers selling insurance and running taxis and spaza shops from schools: 'Our teachers are among the most highly paid in the world in relation to the country's Gross Domestic Product. It's totally inexcusable for any teacher to draw a salary if he is not devoted to his job'. (Govender, 1998)*

> *'New Natal matric shock as headmaster is arrested': KwaZulu Natal came in for another shock this week when the arrest of a headmaster led to the discovery of a well-organised exam fraud which had been operating for several years. The South African Democratic Teachers Union has alleged that pupils had threatened headmasters, teachers and invigilators with death if they did not leak exam papers and allow pupils to crib. (Mahabeer, 1996)*

> *'Mbeki vows to sack bad heads': South Africa's new president has vowed to clamp down on schools that perform poorly. Thabo Mbeki said the government would begin sacking below-par headteachers and sending 'guerrilla units' to conduct spot checks on schools. The government is getting tough with ill-disciplined schools following yet another year when more than 50% of pupils failed school-leaving exams ... 'I am told of instances where, as schools open in the morning, teachers and*

pupils walk to the nearest shebeen and sit drinking', said
Mbeki. Many schools in poor areas are plagued by lack of
discipline and violence. Lessons are offered only occasionally
... There are many examples of excellent schools in poor areas.
But until recently poor performance in disadvantaged schools
was blamed on lack of resources, apartheid curricula and
teacher training and disruption through protest ... Mr. Mbeki
conceded that continued lack of basic infrastructure and
resources was a problem but good teaching was possible in
difficult circumstances he said. (McGregor, 2000a)

'Crash course in chaos shocks the minister': On the first day of
South Africa's new school year, the education minister
descended on a Soweto school with one of the worst records in
the country. Meadowlands high school had a 13% pass rate in
last year's leaving exam, the matric. But when Mr. Asmal
arrived at Meadowlands he found pupils milling in the street,
empty classrooms and teachers absent. Chairs and desks left
outside throughout the Christmas holidays were buried in long
grass. Almost everyone commented on the stench from the
toilets ... He (the minister) blamed the 20 teachers present for a
lack of discipline and organisation. (McGreal, 2000a)

A study of the culture of learning and teaching in Gauteng schools
(Chisholm & Vally, 1996) found that there was concern about the high
levels of absenteeism on the part of teachers and students as well as a
lack of teacher motivation. The principal of one school commented that
teachers did not have a knowledge of what a culture of learning and
teaching might mean, having spent their entire lives in disrupted
schools. He spoke about poor class teaching, no marking and no tests
being given. Students also consistently raised problems of teacher
professionalism. These included lack of respect by teachers for one
another and for students, lack of cooperation, and divisions among
teachers, sexual abuse and harassment of students, use of corporal
punishment and drunkenness. Said one group of students, 'They do not
seem to have a sense of duty and respect for existing regulations.
Teachers are not teachers'. In the foreword to the report, Mary Metcalfe,
the Gauteng provincial minister for education, commented that:

The report is a poignant testimony of the incalculable damage
done to education by apartheid and the enormity of our task of
education reconstruction. Such reconstruction provides an
opportunity to do things anew, to find new and truly
transformatory solutions. The solution is not a panic-driven
return to the external semblances of 'order', the safety of
authoritarianism and rote learning, but the opportunity to

> develop new conceptions of discipline, commitment and
> accountability which are consistent with our new democracy.
> (Chisholm & Vally, 1996, p. i)

Christie (1998) has analysed schools as '(dis)organisations' in the 'poor
and disrupted communities spawned by apartheid'. She notes that the
list of characteristics associated with such schools (absenteeism, low
morale, violence etc.) is an inverse of the 'lists' of features so popular in
effective schools research. Christie uses social psychology and the idea of
'social defence' to analyse and explain the way dysfunctional schools
operate. School organisations need to contain the anxieties associated
with learning and teaching. Rituals, school rules, formalised social
relations and adherence to the boundaries of time and space provide a
form of containment for learners and teachers. However, when the
organisation itself is collapsing – when authority structures have broken
down and the boundaries of time and space no longer exist for staff and
learners – then social defences cannot contain the anxieties of the
organisation's members. She argues that when the organisational context
of schools breaks down, teaching and learning, as basic group tasks in a
school, are subordinated to unconscious group activity whereby social
relations and office politics get more attention than substantive work.
Instead of being able to focus on teaching and learning, schools have
become caught up in forms of conflict, aggression and uncertainty that
cannot be contained in a weak organisational structure. This, she argues,
goes some way to explaining 'the apathy, depression, impotence, anxiety
about physical safety, lack of agency, disempowerment and projection of
blame onto others' that she and other researchers found in the
dysfunctional schools they visited.

However, while it remains true that the legacy of apartheid forms
the specific local context for such schools, particularly in relation to the
levels of crime and violence further discussed below, it also has to be
borne in mind that South Africa is a 'developing country', ranking, for
example, eighty-ninth on the United Nations Human Development Index
(UNDP, 1998). Some of the features of schools discussed above can be
found in all countries, including 'developed' ones, but the pattern and
scale of resource problems, absenteeism, corruption and lack of
professionalism are recurrent issues in the education systems of many
other developing countries. In this wider sense, many South African
schools are not that unusual in that their organisation and management
reflect both the drive for the 'modern', bureaucratic form and the
persistence of pre-modern, economic interests, culture and social
organisation (Harber & Davies, 1997).

Teacher Morale

Since 1994, the Government has taken a number of measures aimed at increasing professionalism and improving the culture of learning and teaching. These have included the introduction of a code of conduct for teachers, a manual for the developmental appraisal of teachers and norms and standards for teacher development. However, these worthwhile initiatives have had to coexist with a situation where teacher morale has not been high:

> *The original intention of the education ministry to effect a*
> *more equitable allocation of resources between rich and poor*
> *schools was severely hampered by budgetary and capacity*
> *constraints. The unintended consequence of teacher*
> *rationalisation, rightsizing and redeployment was a limited*
> *redistribution of educator personnel, the departure of many*
> *committed educators, and insecurity, lack of enthusiasm and*
> *low morale amongst those who chose to continue in teaching.*
> *(Motala et al, 1999, p. 17)*

One study of 354 teachers in the Gauteng area, cited in Vally (1999), found low levels of motivation. Some 68% of teachers who said they were ready to leave the profession were those who opted to stay in service and declined the severance packages the Government offered when it began the rationalisation of public education. Factors undermining morale were violence in schools, resource availability and job security among others. In another survey of 887 teachers in KwaZulu Natal 855 said they regarded teaching as an unattractive career because of the difficult and frustrating conditions, including large class sizes and increased demands by disadvantaged children. Only 27% of the sample felt they had enough time to complete their duties (Moloney, 1998).

Low morale and dissatisfaction has frequently manifested itself in the form of industrial action. During 1998, schools were badly affected by teacher strikes – known in South Africa as a 'chalk down'. On 5 May, for example, 800 teachers were arrested in the Eastern Cape while protesting against the reinstatement of a district official accused of corruption; a march by 12,000 pupils in Thabong in the Free State demanded the reinstatement of retrenched teachers and there was news that over 200 schools in the Durban area would remain closed as a result of disputes between the provincial education department and governing bodies. The South African Democratic Teachers Union (SADTU), the largest teachers' union and traditionally a pro-ANC organisation, in a wide-ranging memorandum to the National Economic, Development and Labour Council accused the Government, among other things of:

– the absence of a culture of delivery and service in the education bureaucracy, including insufficient training and materials for Curriculum 2005;

– lack of proper financial controls leading to overspending and misuse of funds in certain provinces e.g. luxury items, ghost employees, lost textbooks and financing the cost of voluntary severance packages out of the education budget;

– poor logistical management – for example, where textbooks were purchased very poor distribution systems were in place; no means of prioritising needs as resources are distributed on a first come first served basis;

– a perception of inadequate coordination between government departments and between the different levels of departments;

– a need for greater transparency and speedy delivery in the tendering system. (Vally & Spreen, 1998)

Given the difficulties facing South African education in transition outlined above, it is perhaps not surprising that the secondary school matriculation pass rate fell to under 50% (47.1%) in 1997 from 54.7% in 1996. While this was not necessarily a cause for celebration, as the remarks of Thabo Mbeki quoted earlier make clear, it did at least mean that the marking system was intact. As one education journalist put it, 'Given the many problems our schools are facing – that so many experienced teachers have left, that classes are overcrowded, that pupils' numbers are rising, that schools have no textbooks, that the learning atmosphere is wanting – given all these things, a high pass rate would surely give us even more to worry about' (Garson, 1998b).

Effective Schools

School success in examinations is not solely associated with wealth and a high level of resource provision – some schools are successful despite very difficult conditions. Leshata secondary school, for example, is in Orange Farm, an informal settlement south of Johannesburg. It has no library, no computers, no scientific equipment and no musical instruments. There is no electricity in the classrooms because all the junction boxes and fittings have been stolen. The school built a strong room to store the photocopier and typewriters but thieves cut through the thick metal door. Three-quarters of the fathers of the learners are unemployed. The fees, R80 a year, are among the lowest in the country but many parents still find it difficult to pay. Yet, in 1999 Leshata had a

100% pass rate in the matriculation. At nearby Sayaphambili school, not one student passed. The school principal said the success was because the pupils were encouraged to work after regular school hours, which are 7.30 to 2.45 – the school doesn't close until 5.00 pm (McGreal, 2000b).

In 1997, Mafori Mphahele secondary school achieved a 13% pass rate in the matriculation. In 1998, this increased to 65% despite a continuing shortage of textbooks and a lack of matriculation teachers in three key subjects for crucial months of the year. The principal attributed the school's results to a change in the work ethic, commitment and discipline of teachers, parents and pupils. He tightened up on attendance and punctuality, pupils' progress was tracked in order to identify problem areas and he arranged for teachers from local schools to cover lessons that did not have a teacher (Pretorius, 1999).

Mbiliwi school is a rural school where some classrooms are literally crumbling to the ground, water supplies are intermittent and pit toilets must be used, blackboards are falling off the walls, ceilings are rotting, there are too few teachers, there are no computers and textbooks and desks and stationery are scarce. Yet, since 1995 there has been a 100% pass rate at matriculation. A committed headteacher and staff with high expectations is how the success is explained, though because of its success the school is in a position to select one in six pupils on the basis of academic merit (Garson, 1998c).

There is now a very large international literature on school effectiveness and these debates about school effectiveness and school improvement, with their attendant lists of the key characteristics of effective schools, are increasingly influential globally and have certainly arrived in South Africa (Potterton, 1998). However, while the schools cited earlier are obvious examples of effectiveness, British-style league tables based on examination results would clearly be nonsensical in a context where historical disadvantage means enormous disparities between schools. It is also very difficult to say where effectiveness begins and ineffectiveness ends for most schools given the large variety of contexts, histories and combinations of problems. In a rural school with 50% untrained teachers, a large proportion of illiterate parents, no electricity and no running water, would a 20% pass rate be acceptable for the school to rate as effective, whereas in a well-equipped, elite urban school only a 98% pass rate would be acceptable? Or should we judge according to minimum indicators of functional effectiveness – do teachers turn up regularly, is the school reasonably safe, are there enough textbooks? Similarly, the tactics and priorities for school improvement will vary – in some schools it may be that a spirit duplicator is the most important item needed to transform teaching and learning in a situation where there is no electricity. In another school the provision of a permanent headteacher or good security fencing might be more important. However, the three examples of school effectiveness in difficult circumstances cited earlier suggest that while finance and resource provision is not irrelevant, the most urgent priority is one of management and staffing.

An important criticism of the international school effectiveness literature is its tendency to avoid the question of the diversity of goals in education and to assume that examination results are the sole indicator of success. In contrast, it can be argued that ideology is important and that there is no universally agreed on, single set of desirable educational goals or outcomes and that education systems and individual schools can only be judged contextually in terms of the goals they are trying to achieve. In South Africa, as elsewhere, 'effectiveness' cannot be judged solely in terms of examination success. Other important goals for education in South Africa were identified in previous chapters and it is clear that an 'effective school' during the apartheid era could not be judged an effective school now. Just as there are examples of effective schools in terms of success in the matriculation, so there are examples of schools which not only provide an orderly, purposeful and businesslike atmosphere but which also move beyond this to embrace change and to implement a new educational ideology aimed at fostering an inclusive, non-violent, non-racist and democratic South Africa. Examples of these are discussed in Harber & Muthukrishna (forthcoming 2001).

Violence and Education

Owing to a number of historical factors, many South African children were born, reared, have matured, married and died in violent situations. Some have become so immune to violent actions that they see violence as both an acceptable form of expression and as a way of channeling their emotions. Schools located in disadvantaged areas, where the culture of violence reigns, are plagued with violence, crimes, gangs, drugs, contraband and other related problems. (Independent Projects Trust, 1999a, p. 35)

South Africa is a violent society. An average of 52 people were murdered each day in South Africa in 1995, giving it a murder rate more than 80 times that of Britain and making South Africa the most violent country in the world outside a war zone (*Weekly Telegraph*, 20–24 April 1996). In the first 8 months of the same year, 80% of adults and 62% of children faced some sort of violent crime (Morrell, 1998b). A number of factors have combined to cause this 'culture of violence' – over 40 years of gross economic and political inequality, the social dislocation caused by the physical removals of whole communities, violent repression by the apartheid state unavoidably resulting in violent resistance to it, the widespread availability of guns and patriarchal values and behaviours.

Schools have inevitably been affected by violence. The daily press in South Africa regularly contains articles on violence affecting schools, as the following selection of titles of articles indicates: 'Children See Teachers Gunned Down', 'Schools Soft Targets for Gunmen', 'Police Rescue Besieged School from Rampaging Pupils', 'Three in Court over Principal's Shooting' (*The Mercury*, 3 February 1999, 30 August 1999, 17 August 1999 and *The Star*, 27 September 1999). In a survey of 10 schools in Durban (Griggs, 1997), it was found that in nine out of ten, gang-related violence was a major problem and that security measures were seriously inadequate. A quarterly review of education in South Africa noted the irony that:

> *While the world was riveted to media coverage of the horrific*
> *massacre of thirteen high school students in the United States,*
> *the litany of violent acts in South African schools this year*
> *alone far surpassed the tragedy in Colorado. (Vally, 1999, p. 8)*

A review of the existing literature on violence in urban schools in South Africa (Independent Project Trust, 1999a) talks of a 'culture of violence' existing in South African schools – a systemic cycle of violence that had its origin in the apartheid years when institutionalised violence became a way of life in homes, schools and communities. Children grew up in a world surrounded by death, abuse and violence and came to accept it as a way of life. Violence became accepted as a powerful means of attaining change, including change within education, and social status was gained by carrying a gun.

One survey of students in 1991, for example, found that 84% had had one of their schoolmates killed in the political violence and 87% reported having been directly and personally affected by violence while at school (Nzimande & Thusi, 1998). In the townships, violence is exacerbated by poverty and young people often lack self-esteem and personal confidence, so that, in a context where positive role models are few, crime, including violent crime, becomes more attractive. Many South African youth have been victims of violence and are therefore both desensitised and acculturated to it as a way of life. One researcher asked young men within Alexandra township, 'Why is it so easy to kill?' The answer was, 'We are used to people dying. We see death every day, we no longer fear death. To us death has become a way of life' (Motsei, 1998).

While the violence of the surrounding society impinges on schools, often through organised gangs coming on to school premises, schools themselves have also helped to reproduce violence. During the apartheid era, there was direct and deliberate militarisation of schooling. The South African Defence Force was involved in cadet training in white schools from 1976 so that by the late 1980s some 210,000 pupils were involved as an overt preparation for military training in the war to protect apartheid from 'terrorists'. Cadets wore uniforms and were given weapons training. Militarised holiday 'adventure camps' were also organised for coloured and Indian children, essentially indoctrinating the relatively privileged. Participants were encouraged to develop 'leadership, patriotism and military discipline' (Christie, 1991, p. 148).

Schools in South Africa have traditionally been authoritarian institutions stressing obedience, conformity and passivity. The most tangible manifestation of this authoritarianism was the widespread use of officially sanctioned violence against children in the form of corporal punishment (Holdstock, 1990). Corporal punishment is now illegal in South Africa, though it is still commonly used and still supported by many parents and students (Morrell, 1999) and, in KwaZulu Natal, by the Minister of Education herself despite the fact that: 'Numerous studies have shown that, far from curbing violence, corporal punishment in fact encourages antisocial aggression, vandalism and perpetuates the cycle of violence' (Vally, 1999, p. 9).

A recent survey of 750 school students in KwaZulu Natal (Morrell, 1999) found some interesting contradictions. Among African students from township schools in the survey, there was a strong public endorsement of corporal punishment. However, at the same time, the majority of the very same students whose public discourse supported corporal punishment said that they felt anger, hurt and sadness at being wronged in relation to corporal punishment and, almost the opposite, positive feelings about consultative mechanisms of discipline in relation to discussing problems with the teachers in class.

A Culture of Peace and Democracy in Schools?

Chapter 1 described the framework of educational policy that now exists and which sets out to encourage schools to counter the legacy of violence through the promotion of democratic values, human rights and peaceful conflict resolution (Department of Education, 1995a). However, while formal structures of representation may now be established in many schools, it will be more difficult to establish a culture of democratic and peaceful behaviour in schools.

A major criticism of formal schooling is that it overemphasises the cognitive at the expense of the affective, that testable knowledge is somehow separate from and more important than personal understanding and learning how to handle feelings, values, behaviour and relationships. As Ross Epp notes:

> *The purposeful neglect of the personal is fuelled by and*
> *contributes to a dehumanised society. As long as facts, words,*
> *and numbers are treasured and personal feelings are*
> *subverted and discouraged, children will continue to become*

*adults who believe that facts, words and numbers are the most
important aspects of life. (1996, p. 10)*

South Africa is in many ways already a dehumanised society as a result
of its recent oppressive and violent history and there is an urgent need
for social interaction, interpersonal skills, relationships and the affective
to be given equal attention to the cognitive. The remainder of this section
briefly discusses some examples of different approaches where progress
has been made or is being made. All in some way involve an attempt to
prioritise improving the nature of relationships as essential in itself and
as a route to school effectiveness and school improvement in the more
traditional and conventional sense. It must also be noted that the case
study of school democratisation described in chapter 2 would be an
example of an attempt to reduce violence through changing the nature of
relationships in a school.

One interesting example concerns an unusual but seemingly
effective intervention in primary schools in Alexandra township north of
Johannesburg, an area that has been characterised by high levels of crime
and violence as well as drug and alcohol abuse. It brings home the need
to think laterally about solutions sometimes. Here transcendental
meditation was introduced into the school in 1997 by the non-
government agency CIDA (Community and Individual Development
Association). The reported benefits of this focused method of relaxation
are improved concentration and memory, thus enhancing academic
performance, as well a greater sense of control leading to reduced stress
and aggression and a sense of well-being, better behaviour and a
reduction of violence. One student said, 'There are funerals here every
week because of violence and AIDS. There is a lot of violence in other
schools. Since we have been meditating here there is no violence;
children don't fight like they did before. Other schools should meditate'.
The school principal reports improved pass rates at the school, improved
relations between teachers and pupils, higher morale and better
discipline. Other schools in Alexandra using transcendental meditation
have also reported improved pass rates in examinations, better marks in
school subjects, reduced levels of student and teacher absenteeism,
greater success in sports and cultural competitions and reduced levels of
violence, drug and alcohol use (Ewing, 1999).

Another example is the intervention into schooling by non-
governmental organisations, who train staff and students in methods of
peaceful conflict resolution such as negotiation, problem-solving,
communication and peer mediation. This sort of work has been carried
out, for example, by the Centre for Conflict Resolution in Cape Town
(Dovey, 1996) and by the Independent Projects Trust in Durban (Caine &
Matthews, 1998). However, despite evidence that training in peaceful
conflict resolution skills has proved relatively successful in its own
terms (Foulis & Anderson, 1995; Independent Projects Trust, 1997), there

has been an increasing awareness in the Durban-based Independent Projects Trust that this approach is necessary but not sufficient to combat the problem of violence in schools. A significant proportion of violence originates outside the school in the form of intrusions by armed gangs and criminals (Caine & Matthews, 1998). The Independent Projects Trust has therefore played a leading role in facilitating an alliance of public, private and non-governmental organisations, including the police, known as the Community Alliance for Safe Schools (CASS).

The Independent Projects Trust, under the auspices of CASS, has produced a practical guide for school governing bodies on creating a safer school. This takes a more holistic approach and covers such matters as the setting up of a school security committee, writing a security plan, keeping records of incidents, securing the school property, developing a relevant curriculum and the need for more inclusive forms of school management. A key aspect of this is therefore the need to encourage and develop democratic school management and classroom practice in order to create a supportive school environment based on participation, ownership and responsibility so that students are not alienated from the school and thus contribute to the problem (Independent Projects Trust, 1999b). This guide has been used as part of a pilot project with a cluster of three schools in Durban to investigate whether intervention in the form of workshop-based training involving staff, students and parents, coupled with mutual support between the cooperating schools, can reduce crime and violence. An evaluation of the project suggests, encouragingly, that schools are not helpless in the face of crime and violence and that they can be helped to find simple, relatively cheap and practical measures to improve safety and security in quite a short time period (Harber, 2000).

Conclusion

The history of South Africa has left an education system in which there are enormous disparities between schools in terms of resources and levels of professionalism. Post-apartheid educational reform has been applied to a system which is not uniformly positioned to be able to cope successfully with the desired changes. The difficulties of transition have therefore contributed to lower levels of morale among some teachers. Yet, there remain outstanding examples of effective schools, sometimes in the face of very unpromising physical and financial circumstances. More research on what has made these schools successful against the odds would be useful for South African education as a whole. Finally, the high levels of violence existing in South African society have increasingly been recognised as a, if not *the*, major threat to effective schooling. This remains a significant and worrying problem and one that will need to be confronted and tackled in a robust manner. A start has been made but the techniques and lessons learnt so far from small-scale projects designed to enhance school security now urgently need to be publicised, replicated and adapted on a larger scale.

CHAPTER 5

Teacher Education and Teacher Identity

Introduction

*Teacher education in South Africa has always
been characterised by a lack of coherent policy.
(Mokgalane & Vally, 1996, p. 9)*

If post-apartheid educational reform in South Africa is to succeed, the education system will require teachers with new knowledge, skills and values. Initial and in-service teacher education must therefore play an important part in the transformation of the education system. This in turn necessitates a coherent and appropriately structured national teacher education system whose teaching and learning processes are congruent with the need for greater professionalism and the values of the new democratic state. The present chapter therefore examines the nature of teacher education at the inception of democracy in 1994 and the policies that have been introduced subsequently in order to reform the system. However, reform of the education system via teacher education will only work if teachers can be persuaded to adopt the desired new values and practices. This chapter therefore also examines some recent evidence on the identities and value systems of South African teachers.

Teacher Education in 1994

In 1994, the Department of Education commissioned the National Teacher Education Audit, the first and only database on the nature of teacher education in South Africa. It examined 281 teacher education institutions covering a wide range of provision – colleges of education, distance education institutions, universities and technikons (polytechnics), non-governmental organisations involved in teacher education and departmental (governmental) in-service education and training. The report of the audit was made public in December 1995 and some of the main findings were as follows.

- Teacher education (pre-service and in-service) was the largest sector of tertiary education, involving at least 281 organisations and some 490,000 students and educators.
- The teacher education field was also very fragmented with many different types, forms and levels of provision.
- South Africa had sufficient capacity to produce enough teachers for the foreseeable future. In most provinces there was an oversupply of teachers.
- The quality of teacher education was the biggest challenge. The quality of teacher education was generally poor, despite pockets of excellence.
- Good teacher education was rapidly being driven out of existence as more and more institutions turned to cheap correspondence education without student support, instead of high quality open learning.
- There were huge disparities across institutions and sectors as a result of apartheid and the urban/rural divide.
- The existing system of teacher education was inefficient as a result of high failure rates and cost-ineffective institutions.
- The professional mission of teacher education institutions was being subverted by the presence of large numbers of students who had no desire to teach but wanted an affordable route to a higher education qualification.

The audit concluded that insufficient attention had been paid to the quality of teacher education and that system reconstruction was essential:

> *This must include a new conceptual framework and values, new governance and financing arrangements, new curricula focusing on teacher competences, institutional reform, capacity-building and quality assurance mechanisms ... A national policy framework for teacher supply, utilisation and development which coordinates, regulates and synergises the contributions of all the actors is a necessary starting point. (Hofmeyr & Hall, 1996, p. 138)*

The situation in colleges of education was particularly worrying. Under apartheid, colleges were classified as part of the college–school sector rather than higher education and many were established by the so-called homelands or Bantustans. As a result, some 90% of college of education students were of African origin. The dominant approach in the colleges did not reflect the new democratic dispensation and was authoritarian and teacher-centred because of the historical influences of Christian National Education and Fundamental Pedagogics. As a result of apartheid:

*Many colleges have become sites of political contestation and
are pervaded by a set of negative cultures of dependency,
entitlement, resistance to authority and violence. The quality
of teacher education in the sector is very uneven. There are a
range of approaches to teaching and learning, but the
dominant approach is authoritarian and content-based.
Theory and practice are not integrated and neither reflect the
direction of the new South Africa or the latest international
advances in knowledge. However, there are isolated examples
of real innovation and change. (Department of Education,
1995b, p. 52)*

The Reform of Teacher Education

The importance of teacher education in educational reform was signalled
in the new government's *White Paper on Education and Training*:

*The Ministry regards teacher education (including the
professional education of trainers and educators) as one of the
central pillars of national human resource development
strategy, and the growth of professional expertise and self-
confidence is the key to teacher development. (Department of
Education, 1995a, p. 29)*

In terms of the national structure of teacher education, however, planned
change has been slow and uncoordinated until relatively recently. In
1997, colleges of education became institutions of higher education
rather than school-level institutions but a restructuring of the teacher
education sector into a single, coordinated higher education system
waited on a rationalisation of the college sector by the provinces. A sharp
reduction in student demand for places in teacher education, financial
constraints and the existence of too many separate institutions as a result
of apartheid had led to a situation where the number of colleges of
education in the provinces was contracting rapidly. In KwaZulu Natal in
1998, for example, the number of colleges taking a cohort of new
students fell from 17 to six in one year. Demand for initial and in-service
teacher education courses has also declined at many universities and
technikons. Rather than continuing to let teacher education wither on the
vine in an unsystematic way, with many institutions finding it difficult
to plan staffing and levels of provision from one year to the next, the
Government has recently decided on a national programme of
rationalisation and concentration. From 2001, there will be just 25 higher
education institutions involved in teacher education nationally. These
institutions, in many cases representing a merger of existing institutions,
will cater for about 15,000 students, with two distance education
colleges serving another 5000 full-time equivalent students, a reduction

from the situation in 1994 where there were 150 government institutions training about 200,000 students (*Sunday Times*, 23 April 2000).

The body charged with reforming the curriculum or content of teacher education was the Committee on Teacher Education Policy (COTEP). In 1996, COTEP produced its *Norms and Standards for Teacher Education* (COTEP, 1996), which were revised in 1998 (Department of Education, 1998a). The purpose of these documents was to define what was required of a competent teacher in order to reform and evaluate teacher education qualifications. Underpinning the two documents is an overt and strong commitment to education for democracy and human rights – a key aim of teachers is therefore the education of democratic citizens. For example, among the skills cited in the 1996 document as being necessary for a competent teacher are:

- the facilitation of learner-centred classroom practice and collaborative learning;
- the ability to deal with human rights issues, including gender issues;
- the ability to reflect critically on the practice of teaching;
- the ability to reflect critically on education and society; and
- being autonomous, flexible, creative and responsible agents for change in response to the educational challenges of the day and in relation to the espoused aims of education in South Africa.

Among the values stated as being necessary for a competent teacher in the new South Africa were:

- education for critical, responsible and useful citizenship in order to equip the individual for service in the wider community and environment;
- values as encompassed in the human rights manifesto;
- a recognition and understanding of the approaches to multiculturalism; and
- community involvement, promoting adaptability and tolerance in a multicultural society.

It is also important to note, however, that, despite an emphasis on the notion of competence, the COTEP documents do not reflect an adherence to what has become known as 'competency-based teacher education'. A competency-based approach aims to train teachers who, above all else, are skilled and competent classroom technicians and it therefore stresses the importance of teaching skills and behavioural objectives. The emphasis is on learning to do rather than to think. Despite its prevalence in the USA and United Kingdom in the 1980s, and its being the dominant model of teacher education in developing countries (Avalos, 1991), it has been widely criticised. One of the main criticisms is that, while practical training in classroom skills is obviously important, the behavioural approach sees teaching as a neutral, technical and apolitical act and ignores the wider social, political and economic context in which schools and classrooms exist (Popkewitz, 1987; Ginsberg, 1988).

Pendlebury, for example, rejects charges that the COTEP documents are narrowly or crudely behaviouristic in the manner of competency-based teacher education, as:

> *A behaviourist conception assumes the possibility of behavioural outcomes which are open to observation and assessment. Such a conception usually issues in long checklists of evidenced behaviour, as was typical of competency-based teacher education and performance assessment in the USA. The authors of South Africa's Norms and Standards offer no behavioural criteria for 'competencies' nor do they believe that competence can be 'seen' in 'behaviours'. None of the specified competencies can be constructed as mere 'behaviours', since all of them imply agency, intentionality and intelligent action in response to various teaching contexts. (1998, p. 343)*

Instead, she prefers to describe the COTEP approach to competences as general abilities associated with expert performers in a practice or field of activity, where general ability is understood as an aggregate of skills, information and motivation. Indeed, such competencies can be seen as part of an explicit political programme of democracy and development:

> *Appeals to principles of justice, equality and liberty are empty rhetoric and the hard won 'right to learn' is a right with little substance, as long as the education system continues to certificate and employ teachers with shaky subject knowledge or limited professional know-how. Competent teachers are a necessary condition for fulfilment of the right to learn. (1998, p. 345)*

However, even in those institutions with professional and competent staff and a stated commitment to a more democratic approach to teacher education, there are still problems of translating policy into practice. Moletsane (1998) provides a useful case study of the difficulties and contradictions in such a transition. She interviewed staff and sought the views of students on an initial teacher education course at a university Department of Education committed to a more democratic approach. On the one hand, there were more positive signs of democracy than had been the case in South African teacher education in the past. A variety of interactive and participatory teaching and learning methods were used on the course and students were encouraged to analyse critically so that they would be able to teach their learners to do the same. According to both staff and students, racial and cultural tolerance was promoted on the course and teaching and learning methods encouraged and affirmed a plurality of opinions from the diverse group of students in the class. Classes provided an opportunity for self-expression and open debate by students and helped them to find their own voice in a safe and flexible classroom environment. Use of assessment procedures such as projects and continuous assessment marked a move away from formal testing and examinations into methods more based on democratic principles. The accessibility of staff to students minimised hierarchy in relationships, encouraged consultation and allowed students to voice their views freely on both academic and social issues affecting their lives.

On the other hand, there were aspects of the course that did not help to fulfil its democratic aspirations. Within the constraints of increased workloads, it was often necessary for staff to view students as clients who required efficiency and good service for their time and money. According to both staff and students, this led to too much structure in the curriculum and less student involvement in its development. The timetable followed a rigid schedule and allowed very little flexibility in the topics discussed. There was also a mismatch between what the department intended and what the students actually experienced during the school-based aspect of the programme. While the teacher educators expected the students to implement alternative strategies in the classroom, principals and supervising teachers at the schools required the student teachers to maintain the status quo and to teach according to the traditional, teacher-centred paradigm of education. A third issue was that the students do not enter teacher education programmes as blank slates and tend to prefer the same models of teaching and learning that they themselves experienced at school. Efforts to expose the students to alternative methods and approaches were therefore often met with resistance. Finally, while the democratic election of class representatives provided structural space for students' voices in the department, the students were critical of the fact that they were not invited to participate in departmental meetings or any other forum with decision-making powers concerning their course.

Teacher Identity

The entire edifice designed to transform South African education will stand or fall on the basis of support offered to teachers in the implementation of the policy as well as the extent to which the support deals with teacher beliefs and assumptions, and not only the outward signs of practice. (Harley et al, 2000, p. 301)

Teachers are key actors in educational reform in South Africa and elsewhere. Understanding teachers' present beliefs, understanding and practices – their identity – is important if policy implementation is to be successful and if in-service courses are to be suitably designed to facilitate change. While some of these beliefs are discussed below, two immediate concerns must be borne in mind about the role of teachers as agents of change. The first problem is that teachers can be quite unaware of policy developments in the first place. One study, for example, found that on average only 19% of material leaving the national Department of Education actually found its way into the hands of staff and governing bodies (cited in Harley et al, 2000). A second problem is that a commitment to teaching as a profession may not form a strong part of all teachers' personal identity. The National Teacher Education Audit discussed earlier stressed that many students in teacher education colleges did not have a genuine desire to teach and similarly, in a study of teacher voice which included interviews from a sample of 68 South African teachers, more than half attributed purely instrumental reasons related to salary, status, the desire to urbanise and the attainment of qualifications to their choice of teaching as a career. For these teachers, 'the teacher was a person whom socio-economic circumstances had conspired to choose' (Jessop & Penny, 1998, p. 396).

The same study also found that there was considerable nostalgia for an imagined golden age in which children respected elders and certainty prevailed. For some South African teachers, nostalgia for the old order was coupled with suspicion of the new and radical democratic values accompanying the end of apartheid. There were difficulties for some teachers in reconciling the contradictions of the collapse of apartheid (a good thing) with the breakdown of traditional values (a bad thing). This desire for certainty and fixed rules sits awkwardly with one of the key desired outcomes of the new curriculum and one of the key competencies of teacher education as defined by COTEP – the development of creative and critical thinking. Yet, evidence suggests that there remains quite a low level of critical consciousness among teachers. Under apartheid, teachers were expected to follow rules and implement prescriptive curricula established from above. Their job was to obey orders and not to be creative. A study of black teachers in Gauteng in 1994 suggested that the majority of teachers took for granted the structures within which they worked and regarded compliance as necessary for survival and success. The teachers had internalised the modes of thinking and behaviour that had been expected of them under the previous regime. Some of the teachers described, for example, their roles as follows:

> *We are just miserable rule followers ... There is not much that you can do about it ... that's how things have been and they will continue for a long time to come.*

> *Teaching is not treated like a profession because of the controls and administrators on teachers' backs ... We teachers*

generally agree to occupying a subordinate position from which we cannot influence anything within the system. It's always been like this. I don't really plan things for myself.

Being a teacher and the freedom to decide on educational matters are not compatible in this country. (Modiba, 1996)

Related to the need for certainty is a tendency for South African teachers to see knowledge as composed of uncontestable and objective facts to be transmitted for memorisation. Harley et al's study of 10 'effective' teachers at six 'resilient' schools in the Pietermaritzburg education authority in KwaZulu Natal suggested that as a result of this view of knowledge, the teachers were less likely to recognise learners' own experiences as worthwhile resources and to make use of interactive teaching methods such as classroom discussion and debate, therefore closing off most opportunities for developing critical and creative thinking: 'In short, teachers' own epistemologies left them rather uneasily at odds with the requirements of both curriculum and teachers' roles' (2000, p. 295). Another study also identified a tendency for South African teachers to see teaching and learning as 'rules without reasons', memorisation and a fixed view of what constitutes knowledge:

It therefore supports a concept of the teacher and textbook as repositories of expert knowledge, which need to be passed on to pupils unproblematically. Pupils are expected to absorb 'knowledge' in a passive manner, and when assessment demands it, to squeeze the facts out of their sponge-like brains. The focus for pupils and teachers is to know 'the facts' without relation to the reasons for knowing them; essentially, instrumentalism was to know what, without knowing how or why. (Jessop & Penny, 1998, p. 397)

Interestingly, in neighbouring Namibia, which has begun a process of democratic post-apartheid reform of education similar to that of South Africa (Harber, 1997a; Angula & Grant Lewis, 1997), a study of a group of teacher educators found that they held similar views of knowledge. They held the strong belief that for any course of study there ought to be a pre-specified body of knowledge and/or skills which had been identified by the instructor. The task of the instructor was to utilise appropriate media to facilitate a step-by-step accumulation of this knowledge by the learners. For these teacher educators, knowledge was independent of people and context and seen as objective and the group was thrown off-balance by the suggestion that they might have ideas which would both count as knowledge and be valuable in a learning situation (Rowell, 1995).

Finally, even when teachers are well aware of and understand the requirements of government policy, they may disagree with it and prefer their own views, beliefs and experience as a basis for behaviour and action. The study by Harley et al, for example, found that teachers' comments reflected some of the practical complexities arising from the contradictions between policy expectations and the culture and personal value systems of the teachers. When asked by a researcher whether he personally believed in gender equality, one teacher, a union official and knowledgeable about the rights of teachers and learners, said, 'Never ever! As a man, I believe I am and will always be superior to a woman. Our culture is consistent with this view'. There was also some resistance to the Government's promotion of the role of teacher as a key person in community development, and six out of ten of the teachers taught at schools that still used corporal punishment, despite the fact that it was illegal. There was also some active resistance to the idea of pupils as critical learners:

> *The new policy is good but there will be conflict between*
> *the government and the Zulu rural community. If children*
> *become more critical they will start to question their parents'*
> *authority and adopt values that conflict with their community.*
> *(2000, pp. 295–296)*

Conclusion

In order to achieve the educational reform desired in government policy, South Africa requires a very different type of teacher from that encouraged under apartheid. Not only does this mean competent and professional teachers but also teachers ideologically committed to democratic values and skilled in democratic forms of teaching and learning. This presents a serious challenge to institutions concerned with initial teacher education in helping to shape the democratic teaching force of the future. However, given the evidence on existing patterns of teacher identity described in this chapter and the general problems faced by South African education that have been discussed in this book, it is obvious that government policy reform is no longer the priority. To move from policy to implementation and for educational reform to begin to stand a chance of succeeding, the overwhelming and urgent need is for widespread, appropriate and coordinated forms of in-service professional development for existing teachers.

Conclusion: no instant miracles – from policy to practice

The term 'transition' implies a destination or goal – a transition *to* something. Since the collapse of communism and the end of the cold war in the late 1980s, two main ideological destinations have predominated globally. One, numerically in the minority, has been Islamicisation of the state and the education system. Iran has been a model for this process, though the aim is also being pursued by the Government of Sudan, by the Taliban in Afghanistan and political movements in, for example, Algeria and northern Nigeria. Numerically more significant internationally has been the pursuit of democracy as the goal of political development. A wide range of states in Africa, Latin America, Asia and eastern Europe once characterised by one-party or military systems of government have begun a transition, however gradual and flawed, to a more democratic form of government. Some of the pressure for this has been internally generated by dissatisfaction with the brutality and generally poor economic and social performance of authoritarian regimes. Pressure for democratic reform, however, has also come externally from global organisations such as the World Bank and the various aid agencies of European and North American governments.

Despite the messy contradictions and setbacks that such attempted transitions can entail in practice, this variant of globalisation, with its emphasis on human rights, pluralism and social and political equality, is to be generally welcomed. Moreover, a key aspect of the process of the transition to democracy has been a long overdue attempt to reform education systems in a democratic direction in order to educate young people with the values and skills they will need as democratic citizens. South Africa is clearly in this latter camp and has clearly set itself on this path of transition to a democratic political system and society, with education being identified as a key mechanism in this process. However, financial and resource constraints, in a context where education is now to be provided equally to all, means that transition in education is a slow and difficult process.

As this book has outlined, the 6 years since the end of apartheid have seen dramatic and largely constructive changes in educational policy affecting such areas as funding, management, curriculum and social equality – all aimed at the eventual creation of a more democratic society. The policy framework for education in the new South Africa is now firmly in place and it is doubtful whether schools and teachers would readily welcome any major new policy initiatives for the time being. On one occasion in South Africa when I complained to a South African colleague about the lack of vision and imagination in British educational policy as opposed to South African education policy, his reply was to the effect, 'Yes, but at least you know there that it is actually likely to happen'. South African education now needs a lengthy period of consolidation and implementation. However, the size of the barriers to implementing reform policies on the ground remain dauntingly high:

- the deep-rooted and persistent nature of old values and behaviours based on inequality such as racism and sexism;
- the violence that permeates South African society and its schools;
- the persistence of violent forms of punishment;
- the patchy and inconsistent nature of professionalism amongst South African teachers;
- low morale amongst teachers;
- teacher identities and priorities at odds with the direction of educational reform;
- the overcomplex, centralised and rushed nature of some of the reforms themselves;
- the variation in competence and efficiency between provinces in terms of their capability to deliver genuine change;
- the growing threat to educational stability posed by the AIDS crisis;
- the complex linguistic heritage;
- the extreme resource disparities between schools; and
- insufficient in-service teacher education and doubts about the nature and quality of initial teacher education.

Such barriers help to account for the wide gap between policy and practice, between the real and the ideal in South African education. Yet, as this book has shown, there are also many examples of good practice and positive innovation to be found operating in South African education. It is important to publicise and to learn from these and the important question is how to use these local examples, and existing international experience, to spread a new democratic professionalism or transformational competence widely among South African educators and educational administrators. One answer is through a more focused and comprehensive effort at the professional in-service development of existing educators and the production of committed and competent teachers from initial training courses. However, this is likely to be a long and slow process, as providing the in-service education of serving teachers on the scale and intensity required would be a very expensive undertaking. Funding such an undertaking by borrowing from an organisation like the World Bank brings its own conditions and may well end up being counter-productive (Harber, 1997c). In the meantime, in order to begin to bridge the gap between policy and practice there may well be a need to look at the other end of the relationship and to reconsider, simplify and clarify some existing policy, including the relationship between the central ministry and provincial responsibility for education.

It is clear that there have not been any instant miracles or quick fixes in South African education. The aim is longer term transformation to democracy and the next key stage is to move from policy to practice. Of course, writing now from a British-based perspective, it is salutary to remember that Britain began its transition to democracy some eight hundred years ago in 1215 and has still got nowhere near eliminating bigotry and racism, let alone democratising its education system. In my opinion at least, the general direction set by South African policy-makers is the best one available but it is to be hoped that the goals can be achieved in something of a shorter timescale than the United Kingdom has managed to date.

References

Angula, N. & Grant Lewis, S. (1997) Promoting Democratic Processes in Educational Decision Making: reflections from Namibia's first five years, *International Journal of Educational Development*, 17, pp. 233–250.

Avalos, B. (1991) *Approaches to Teacher Education: initial teacher education*. London: Commonwealth Secretariat.

Azuma, H. (1999) *The Implications of Public School Fees for Educational Performance and Enrolment with Reference to the Greater Durban Area*, unpublished M.Ed dissertation, University of Natal, Durban.

Badcock-Walters, P. (2000) *AIDS Brief for Sectoral Planners and Managers: Education Sector*. Durban: USAID.

Broughton, T. (2000) School Racism a Big Issue, Says HRC, *The Mercury*, 7 April.

Brown, D. (1998) Governing Bodies Decide on Language Policy, in J. Hofmeyr & H. Perold (Eds) *Education Africa Forum*. Gauteng: Education Africa.

Caine, G. & Matthews, I. (1998) Education for Conflict Resolution in Kwa-Zulu Natal, South Africa, in C. Harber (Ed.) *Voices for Democracy: a North–South dialogue on education for sustainable democracy*. Nottingham: Education Now in Association with the British Council.

Carrim, N. (1998) Anti-racism and the 'New' South African Educational Order, *Cambridge Journal of Education*, 28, pp. 301–320.

Chisholm, L. (1995) A Review of the Year, *Quarterly Review of Education and Training in South Africa*, 2, pp. 1–19.

Chisholm, L. & Fuller, B. (1996) Remember People's Education? Shifting Alliances, State-building and South Africa's Narrowing Policy Agenda, *Journal of Education Policy*, 11, pp. 693–716.

Chisholm, L. & Petersen, T. (1999) Education Policy and Practice on the Eve of the 99 Election, *Quarterly Review of Education and Training in South Africa*, 6, pp. 1–15.

Chisholm, L. & Vally, S. (1996) *The Culture of Learning and Teaching in Gauteng Schools*. Johannesburg: University of Witwatersrand Education Policy Unit.

Christie, P. (1991) *The Right to Learn*. Johannesburg: SACHED/Raven.

Christie, P. (1998) Schools as (Dis)Organisations: the 'breakdown of the culture of learning and teaching' in South African schools, *Cambridge Journal of Education*, 28, pp. 283–300.

Committee on Teacher Education Policy (COTEP) (1996) *Norms and Standards for Teacher Education*. Pretoria: COTEP.

Cowen, R. (1999) Late Modernity and the Rules of Chaos: an initial note on transitologies and rims, in R. Alexander, P. Broadfoot & D. Phillips (Eds) *Learning from Comparing*. Oxford: Symposium Books.

de Clercq, F. (1997) Effective Policies and the Reform Process: an evaluation of the new development and education macro policies, in P. Kallaway, G. Kruss, A. Fataar & G. Donn (Eds) *Education after Apartheid*. Cape Town: University of Cape Town Press.

Department of Education (1995a) White Paper on *Education and Training* (Pretoria).

Department of Education (1995b) *National Teacher Education Audit: Synthesis Report* (Pretoria).

Department of Education (1996) *South African Schools Bill* (Pretoria).

Department of Education (1997a) *Understanding the Schools Act* (Pretoria).

Department of Education (1997b) *Curriculum 2005. Lifelong Learning for the 21st Century* (Pretoria).

Department of Education (1997c) *Curriculum 2005. Discussion Document on Specific Outcomes, Assessment Criteria and Range Statements Grades 1–9* (Pretoria).

Department of Education (1997d) *School Register of Needs Survey* (Pretoria).

Department of Education (1998a) *Norms and Standards for Teacher Education* (Pretoria).

Department of Education (1998b) *Assessment Policy in the General Education and Training Band Grade R and ABET* (Pretoria).

Dovey, V. (1996) Exploring Peace Education in South African Settings, *Peabody Journal of Education*, 71, pp. 128–150.

Dyanti, A. (1999) No Sex Education, Please ... Teachers Walk out of AIDS Lecture, *Saturday Star*, 31 July.

Ewing, D. (1999) Changing the World from Within, *Children First*, February/March.

Fearnly, F. (1998) Impressions from a Township School (unpublished memo).

Foulis, C-A. & Anderson, D. (1995) *Evaluation of the SMART Programme with the IPT*. Durban: Olive.

Fullan, M. (1991) *The New Meaning of Educational Change*. London: Cassell.

Gardiner, M. (1999) Education and Innovation: rethinking the familiar, *Quarterly Review of Education and Training in South Africa*, 6, pp. 1–19.

Garson, P. (1998a) Teacher Redeployment: what went wrong? in J. Hofmeyr & H. Perold (Eds) *Education Africa Forum*. Gauteng: Education Africa.

Garson, P. (1998b) Things Could Be Worse, *The Teacher*, February.

Garson, P. (1998c) The Sweet Smell of Success, *The Teacher*, October.

Garson, P. (1999) At the End of the Rainbow, *Mail and Guardian*, 12–18 March.

Ginsburg, M. (1988) *Contradictions in Teacher Education and Society*. Lewes: Falmer Press.

Govender, P. (1998) Crackdown on Errant Teachers, *Sunday Times*, 10 May.

Graham-Brown, S. (1991) *Education in the Developing World*. New York: Longman.

Greenstein, R. (1995) New Policies, Old Challenges: reshaping the education system *Quarterly Review of Education and Training in South Africa*, 3, pp. 1–11.

Greenstein, R. (1997) New Policies and the Challenges of Budgetary Constraints, *Quarterly Review of Education and Training in South Africa*, 4, pp. 1–12.

Griggs, R. (1997) *Children at Risk: the security situation in Durban schools*. Durban: Independent Projects Trust.

Harber, C. (1996) *Small Schools and Democratic Practice*. Nottingham: Educational Heretics Press.

Harber, C. (1997a) *Education, Democracy and Political Development in Africa*. Brighton: Sussex Academic Press.

Harber, C. (1997b) International Developments and the Rise of Education for Democracy, *Compare*, 27, pp. 171–191.

Harber, C. (1997c) Markets, Equity and Democracy – structural adjustment and the tensions of educational change in South Africa, *International Journal of Educational Development*, 18, pp. 247–254.

Harber, C. (1998) Desegregation, Racial Conflict and Education for Democracy in the New South Africa: a case study of institutional change, *International Review of Education*, 44, pp. 569–582.

Harber, C. (2000) Protecting Your School from Crime and Violence: skills for creating a safe school – evaluation of a one year programme facilitated by the IPT. Durban: Unpublished Report for IPT.

Harber, C. & Davies, L. (1997) *School Management and Effectiveness in Developing Countries: the post-bureaucratic school*. London: Cassell.

Harber, C. & Muthukrishna, N. (2001) School Effectiveness and School Improvement in Context: the case of South Africa, *School Effectiveness and School Improvement* – forthcoming.

Harley, K., Barasa, B., Bertram, C., Mattson, E. & Pillay, S. (2000) The Real and the Ideal: teacher roles and competences in South African policy and practice, *International Journal of Educational Development*, 20, pp. 287–304.

Hofmeyr, J. & Hall, G. (1996) The National Teacher Education Audit, *Perspectives in Education*, 17, pp. 135–140.

Holdstock, T. (1990) Violence in Schools: discipline, in B. McKendrick & W. Hoffman (Eds) *People and Violence in South Africa*. Oxford: Oxford University Press.

Independent Projects Trust (IPT) (1997) *Annual Report for Period March 1997–March 1998 for SMART Project*. Durban: IPT.

Independent Projects Trust (IPT) (1999a) *Protecting Your School from Violence and Crime: guidelines for principals and school governing bodies*. Durban: IPT.

Independent Projects Trust (IPT) (1999b) *The Experience Review of Interventions and Programmes Dealing with Youth Violence in Urban Schools in South Africa*. Durban: IPT.

Jansen, J. (1997) Essential Alterations? A Critical Analysis of the State's Syllabus Revision Process, *Perspectives in Education*, 17(2), pp. 1–11.

Jansen, J. (1998) Curriculum Reform in South Africa: a critical analysis of outcomes-based education, *Cambridge Journal of Education*, 28, pp. 321–332.

Jessop, T. & Penny, A. (1998) A Study of Teacher Voice and Vision in the Narratives of Rural South African and Gambian Primary School Teachers, *International Journal of Educational Development*, 18, pp. 393–404.

Kallaway, P. (Ed.) (1984) *Apartheid and Education*. Johannesburg: Ravan Press.

Kallaway, P., Kruss, G., Fataar, A. & Donn, G. (Eds (1997) *Education after Apartheid*. Cape Town: University of Cape Town Press.

Karlsson, J., McPherson, G. & Pampallis, J. (1999) A Critical Examination of the Evolution and Development of the Policy for School Governance in Public Schools, unpublished paper, Education Policy Unit, Natal and Centre for Education Policy Development, Johannesburg.

Kgobe, M. (1996) Realising Change: the continuing process of policy development and implementation, *Quarterly Review of Education and Training in South Africa*, 4.

MacGregor, K. (2000a) Mbeki Vows to Sack Bad Heads, *Times Educational Supplement*, 21 January.

MacGregor, K. (2000b) Baffling Curriculum Dropped, *Times Educational Supplement*, 23 June.

Macpherson, G. (1998) Report on a Primary Farm School in a Rural Area, unpublished research for the Centre for Educational Policy Development, Johannesburg.

Mandela, N. (1994) *Long Walk to Freedom*. London: Little, Brown.

Mahabeer, G. (1996) New Natal Matric Shock as Headmaster Arrested, *Sunday Times*, 17 November.

Martin, D. (1997) Towards a New Multilingual Language Policy in Education in South Africa: different approaches to meet different needs, *Educational Review*, 49, pp. 129–139.

McGreal, C. (1999) Child Rape Shock for South Africa's Establishment, *Guardian*, 8 September.

McGreal, C. (2000a) Crash Course in Chaos Shocks the Minister, *Guardian*, 1 February.

McGreal, C. (2000b) A School Triumphs Amid the Shacks, *Guardian*, 1 February.

McLean, D. (1998) An Introduction to the South African National Qualifications Framework, in J. Hofmeyr & H. Perold (Eds) *Education Africa Forum*. Gauteng: Education in Africa.

McLeish, W. (1998) Processes of Educational Transition in Countries Moving from Authoritarian Rule to Democratic Government, in E. McLeish & D. Phillips (Eds) *Process of Transition in Education Systems*, Oxford Studies in Comparative Education. Oxford: Symposium Books.

Mkhatshwa, S. (1997) Speech delivered at Culture of Learning, Teaching and Service Campaign Consultative Conference, 22–24 August.

Modiba, M. (1996) South African Black Teachers' Perceptions about Their Practice, *Perspectives in Education*, 17, pp. 117–134.

Mokgalane, E. & Vally, S. (1996) Between Vision and Practice: policy processes and implementation, *Quarterly Review of Education and Training in South Africa*, 3, pp. 1–19.

Moletsane, R. (1998) Towards Democratic Teacher Education in South Africa: an exploratory case study, in C. Harber (Ed.) *Voices for Democracy: a North–South dialogue of education for sustainable democracy*. Nottingham: Education Now in Association with the British Council.

Moloney, K. (1998) Teachers' Morale the Lowest, *The Mercury*, 15 September.

Morrell, R. (1998a) Of Boys and Men: masculinity and gender in Southern African studies, *Journal of Southern African Studies*, 24, pp. 605–630.

Morrell, R. (1998b) Gender and Education: the place of masculinity in South African schools, *South African Journal of Education*, 18, pp. 218–225.

Morrell, R. (1999) Beating Corporal Punishment: race, masculinity and educational discipline in the schools of Durban, South Africa, paper presented at the Voices in Gender and Education Conference, Warwick, UK, March.

Motala, S. (1998) Reviewing Education Policy and Practice: constraints and responses, *Quarterly Review of Education and Training in South Africa*, 5, pp. 1–24.

Motala, S., Vally, S. & Modiba, M. (1999) A Call to Action: a review of Minister K. Asmal's educational priorities, *Quarterly Review of Education and Training in South Africa*, 6, pp. 1–34.

Motsei, M. (1998) Experience of Violence amongst Young Black Men in Alexandra, unpublished paper. Alexandra: ADAPT (Agisanang Domestic Abuse Prevention and Training).

Naidoo, J. (1996) *Racial Integration of Public Schools in South Africa*. Durban: Education Policy Unity, University of Natal.

Nkomo, M. (Ed.) (1990) *Pedagogy of Domination*. Trenton: Africa World Press.

Nzimande, B. & Thusi, S. (1998) Children of War: the impact of political violence on schooling in KwaZulu Natal, in *Democratic Governance of Public Schooling in South Africa*. Durban: University of Natal Education Policy Unit.

Pendlebury, S. (1998) Transforming Teacher Education in South Africa: a space–time perspective, *Cambridge Journal of Education*, 28, pp. 333–350.

Pillay, C. (2000a) Call for AIDS impact study, *The Mercury*, 20 April.

Pillay, C. (2000b) Education System Warned on Rampant Spread of AIDS, *The Mercury*, 5 April.

Popkewitz, T. (Ed.) (1987) *Critical Studies in Teacher Education*. Lewes: Falmer Press.

Potterton, M. (1998) What Makes Schools Effective? in J. Hofmeyr & H. Perold (Eds) *Education Africa Forum*. Gauteng: Education Africa.

Pretorius, C. (1999) Miracle Results at Poor School, *Sunday Times*, 3 January.

Randall, E. (1999) Discrimination to Be Outlawed, *Sunday Independent*, 14 February.

Ratshitanga, M. (1998) The Victims of Racism Speak Out, *The Teacher*, March.

Ross Epp, J. (Ed.) (1996) *Systemic Violence: how schools hurt children.* London: Falmer Press.

Rowell, P. (1995) Perspectives on Pedagogy in Teacher Education: the case of Namibia, *International Journal of Educational Development*, 15, pp. 3–13.

Russell, E. (1998) A Study of the Curriculum Processes and Practices of the Participants Involved in the Implementation of Outcomes-based Education, unpublished M.Ed dissertation, University of Natal, Durban.

Samoff, J. (Ed.) (1994) *Coping with Crisis: austerity, adjustment and human resources.* London: Cassell.

Sayed, Y. (1999) Discourses on the Policy of Educational Decentralisation in South Africa since 1994: an examination of the South African Schools Act, *Compare*, 29, pp. 141–152.

Serote, P. (1992) Solomon Mahlangu Freedom College: a unique South African educational experience in Tanzania, *Transformation*, 20, pp. 55–66.

Sithole, S. (1998) The Participation of Students in Democratic School Governance, in Education Policy Unit, Natal *Democratic Governance of Public Schooling in South Africa.* Durban: EPU, University of Natal.

Skuy, M. & Vice, H. (1996) Attitudes of White Teachers towards Racial Integration in South Africa, *Educational Research*, 38, pp. 135–146.

Soobrayan, B. (1998) People's Education for People's Power, in Education Policy Unit, Natal *Democratic Governance of Public Schooling in South Africa.* Durban: EPU, University of Natal.

United Nations Development Programme (1998) *Human Development Report.* Oxford: Oxford University Press.

USAID (1997) *Education Decentralisation in Africa.* Washington: USAID.

Vally, S. (1999) Teachers in South Africa: between fiscal austerity and getting learning right, *Quarterly Review of Education and Training in South Africa*, 6.

Vally, S. & Dalamba, Y. (1999) *Racism, 'Racial Integration' and Desegregation in South African Public Secondary Schools.* Johannesburg: South African Human Rights Commission.

Vally, S. & Spreen, C-A. (1998) Education Policy and Implementation Developments, *Quarterly Review of Education and Training in South Africa*, 5, pp. 1–22.

Vulliamy, G. (1981) The Secondary Schools Extension Project, *Journal of Curriculum Studies*, 13, pp. 93–102.

Wedekind, V., Lubisi, C., Harley, K. & Gultig, J. (1996) Political Change, Social Integration and Curriculum: a South African case study, *Journal of Curriculum Studies*, 28, pp. 419–436.

Welgemoed, A. (1998) Democratising a School in South Africa, in C. Harber (Ed.) *Voices for Democracy: a North–South dialogue on education for sustainable democracy*. Nottingham: Education Now in association with the British Council.

Wolpe, H. (1995) The Struggle against Apartheid Education: towards people's education in South Africa, in V. McKay (Ed.) *A Sociology of Educating*. Johannesburg: Lexicon Publishers.

Wolpe, A-M., Quinlan, O. & Martinez, L. (1997) *Gender Equity in Education: report of the Gender Equity Task Team*. Pretoria: Department of Education.

Zafar, S. (1998) School-based Initiatives to Address Racial and Cultural Diversity in Newly Integrating Public Schools. Durban: Research Report, Education Policy Unit, University of Natal.